# FIRE YOUR BOSS

# FIRE
## YOUR
# BOSS

STEPHEN  M. POLLAN

A N D

MARK LEVINE

HarperResource

*An Imprint of* **HarperCollins***Publishers*

HarperCollins books may be purchased for educational, business, or sales promotional use. For information please write: Special Markets Department, HarperCollins Publishers Inc., 10 East 53rd Street, New York, NY 10022.

**FIRST EDITION**

*Designed by Richard Oriolo*

LIBRARY OF CONGRESS CATALOGING-IN-PUBLICATION DATA

Pollan, Stephen M.
   Fire your boss / by Stephen M. Pollan and Mark Levine.
     p. cm.
   Includes index.
   ISBN 0-06-058393-2
   1. Career changes. 2. Career development. 3. Self-actualization (Psychology) I. Levine, Mark, 1958– II. Title.

HF5384.P6474 2004
650.14—dc22

2004040538

04 05 06 07 08 WBC/RRD 10 9 8 7 6 5 4 3 2 1

For Ruthellen,

who fired her boss and hired herself years

before we thought of it.


For Molly,

who always knew she was the boss.

# ACKNOWLEDGMENTS

Thanks to Dave Conti and Megan Newman for helping us remain focused on our readers' needs. Thanks to Stuart Krichevsky for knowing there's no I in agent. Thanks to the clients of Stephen M. Pollan for letting us fish for details in their life stories. And thanks to Corky Pollan and Deirdre Martin Levine for helping us live the lives of our dreams.

# CONTENTS

# PART I

# THE FIRE YOUR
# BOSS PHILOSOPHY

# CHAPTER 1

# The Job of Your Dreams

*Your vision will become clear only when you can look
into your own heart. Who looks outside, dreams;
who looks inside, awakes.*

—CARL JUNG

YOU CAN TAKE charge of your work life.

Are you like the office manager wishing she could spend more time at home caring for her children than at the office catering to a juvenile boss?

Are you like the regional manager worrying that the new hotshot vice president of sales will fire him two years short of his daughter's finishing college?

You don't have to accept your current work situation. You can be in control of your job and your stream of income so you're never again subject to the whims, prejudices, moods, or circumstances of your so-called boss. It doesn't matter whether you've been on the job for forty years or forty days; it's never too late or too early to seize control of your work life. It doesn't matter if you're a stock clerk at a video store or the chief financial officer of a movie studio; everyone who's employed can take charge of his or her own work life. I won't lie to you: becoming boss of your own life is neither quick nor easy. The program I outline in this book will require hard work and real thought. It's not something you can do in a weekend. But, believe me, it's worth the time and effort.

Being master of your own work life leads to incredible changes in your life. You'll earn more money if that's what you wish. You'll feel more secure if that's your goal. You'll be able to pursue whatever brings you the most joy and satisfaction, whether it's having a catch with your son, puttering around in the garden, or serving meals to the needy. You'll end up with the job of your dreams, and that will give you a leg up on living the life of your dreams. Just ask Sydney Carton.

Sydney is now sleeping well at night. For years, however, he lay awake worrying. He worried about the state of his career; whether he'd ever achieve his life's dreams; how he'd pay for his daughter's college education; and whether he and his wife, Lucy, would ever be able to retire. He worried about when they'd actually get to spend some quality time together as a family with all the hours he and his wife were working. But Sydney is not worried anymore. His income is fine—he's not an NBA first-round draft pick, but he's doing okay. His job is as secure as it can be in today's world because his boss depends on him more than ever. And even with that security, he's spending less time at work and more at home. He has taken up photography again. He and Lucy have rekindled their romance, thanks to being able to spend time together. And he's being the kind of father he always wanted to be. Sydney turned his work life around . . . and so can you.

You can find a new job that pays an income large enough to keep pace with your family's needs and wants.

You can find a new job with the kind of security that lets you sleep soundly and not lie awake worrying about money.

You can find a new job that lets you achieve the emotional and psychological satisfaction you've always sought.

And you can do all this without getting more education or training, without moving, without changing industries. You don't need to learn a new style of résumé, memorize new buzzwords to drop into your conversations, or learn the latest variations of job hunting.

In fact, you may not need to find a new job at all.

I know this sounds crazy. It flies in the face of what everyone is saying. The media are filled with stories about how the American job market has permanently turned into a cold, chaotic, and corrupt environment. The world of paternalistic companies and loyal employees is extinct, say the pundits. It's a dog-eat-dog world today, in which every man and woman has to be out for him- or herself. We're told we've become a nation of mercenaries engaged in a Darwinian struggle in which only the fittest survive and get to keep their jobs.

Setting all the overblown rhetoric aside, it's clear that the American workplace has changed. More and more full-time jobs are being turned into part-time or contingent positions. Back-office operations are being outsourced. Instead of staff being added, temps are hired. There's no more climbing up a company ladder. Upper-level positions are filled with outsiders stolen from competitors, and to move up at all you've got to first move out. To keep your job it used to be enough to show up on time, do your job for eight hours, and go home. Today you're expected to work for as long as it takes to do your work . . . and the work of the two people who were laid off last month. (See the box on page 6: How Long Are You Working?)

But I'm not telling you anything you don't know already. You've probably seen firsthand signs of the new job market. I bet there are empty desks at work where longtime productive coworkers used to sit before they were laid off. There are probably some people in your office who have shifted over to part-time in an effort to keep their jobs.

## HOW LONG ARE YOU WORKING?

It's not just in your head. If you're anything like the rest of Americans, you are indeed working longer hours than ever. According to the Economic Policy Institute, the average middle-income married couple with children is now working 660 hours more per year than in 1979, the equivalent of more than sixteen extra weeks of full-time work. In 2000, American workers worked an average of 1,877 hours. That's more than in any other rich industrialized nation. To see how your hours measure up, fill in this quick worksheet:

1. What time do you arrive at work? _____

2. What time do you leave work? _____

3. How many hours does that add up to each day? _____

4. How many days a week do you go to the office? _____

5. How many hours does that add up to each week? _____

6. How many days a week do you go out for lunch? _____

7. How long do spend at lunch when you go out? _____

8. How many hours does that add up to each week? _____

If you're like most of us, you're working longer and longer hours, without getting more pay, because you've been sent a veiled message that unless you bite the bullet you'll be out of a job. Friends may be coming to you asking for leads because they've been out of work and are unable to land a new job. Maybe you're out of work yourself, or just losing sleep, playing out worst-case scenarios in your head.

Despite the rhetoric and all the doom and gloom around you, I believe you have an incredible opportunity right now to turn your work life around and create the perfect job situation.

9. Subtract line 8 from line 5 for total hours at the job.     _____

10. How many hours of work do you bring home weekly?     _____

11. How many hours do you go into the office on the weekend?     _____

12. Add line 10 and line 11 for time spent working off the job.     _____

13. Add line 12 to line 9 for hours worked weekly.     _____

14. How many weeks of vacation do you get?     _____

15. Subtract line 14 from 52 for weeks worked yearly.     _____

16. Multiply line 15 by line 13 for hours worked.     _____

If you want to get an even more accurate appraisal of how much of your life is devoted to work, add the number of hours you spend commuting to and from the job to the number on line 13 and go through the subsequent steps again.

You can achieve job security, even in a market in which everyone has become a job hopper and at a time when job tenure has been dropping.

You can maintain all the benefits and higher pay of full-time employment, even in a market in which everyone has become a contingency worker and at a time when temps seem the only permanent workers.

You can survive and thrive at work, and still have time for a personal life, even in a market that requires long hours and putting the company first.

You can create a solid, secure stream of income and use it to fuel a happy life.

What all the pundits and experts can't see, and what you haven't been told (until now) is that landing the job of your dreams has little to do with your company, your boss, your profession, or your location. It has nothing to do with your résumé, your expanding menu of job skills, or your impressive business Rolodex. Sure, the state of the economy makes a difference, but it's not the most important factor. Landing the job of your dreams is an *inside job*. It's done by adopting an entirely new attitude toward work and the workplace, one that puts you in charge of your job. The trick is to "fire your boss" and replace him or her yourself. I know it works because I see it happen firsthand, day after day, in my office.

## In the Belly of the Beast

My name is Stephen M. Pollan. I'm an attorney and life coach. In the more than two decades I've been a personal consultant, I've helped hundreds of people land the job of their dreams. And I've continued to do that in the past couple of years, during what all the experts say is a horrible job climate, in what those same experts say is one of the worst job markets in America: New York City.

I have a unique practice. I take what, for lack of a better term, I call a holistic approach to my clients' money lives. I believe it's vital to look at financial and work decisions in context. For example, I have new clients get complete medical checkups before we launch into long-term planning, since there's no point in taking steps to financially prepare for a long life unless you're taking care of your health as well. I ask clients about their relationship and parenting needs and wants, since I think it's essential for job and family to mesh as smoothly as possible. When I meet with clients, we talk about investing, relationships, real estate, insurance, wishes for parents and children, personal spending, work problems and goals, hobbies, and life dreams. I believe a comprehensive, all-embracing approach to both life and work offers the greatest rewards. I don't adhere to any particular school of investing, believe in any one philosophy of business, or preach a specific approach to real estate. All I care about is helping my clients set their goals, and then achieve them. Because my clients' success is my sole aim, and because my holistic approach requires me to deal with very personal issues, I get quite wrapped up in my clients' lives.

The past three years have been very traumatic for my clients and me. Most of my clients live and/or work in New York City. The attacks of September 11 and their lingering aftermath offer physical and psychological reminders of the impermanence of modern life. A local economy already reeling from the bursting of the Internet stock balloon suffered even more damage on September 11. Up until then most of my clients had been feeling secure at work. Sure, there were crises in individual companies or industries that led to terminations, but the economy overall was strong enough to create other job openings. And many of my clients, having spent the 1980s and 1990s turning "networking" into a lifestyle, were expert at landing new jobs. In the past three years, however, those tried and true techniques they had mastered suddenly stopped working. That's when they came to me for help.

Confronted with clients in need, and not having any deeply held allegiance to the traditional rules for finding jobs and thriving in the workplace, I started working with my clients to develop new techniques. Since all I, and they, care about is whether the approach works, we felt free to pursue contrarian and iconoclastic ideas. The result is an admittedly radical new seven-step approach to work that flies in the face of conventional wisdom.

## Fire Your Boss . . . and Hire Yourself

The essential first step in winning the job of your dreams is to fire your boss . . . and hire yourself. In other words, you need to stop letting your boss, or company, or anyone else for that matter, dictate the course of your work life, and take charge of your own present and future. It's ironic, but Americans, who are usually so obsessed with taking charge of large and small aspects of their lives, cede control of their work lives to others.

Think I'm overstating the case? Let's go back to the beginning of your work life to see how much control you've given away. What did you major in when you were at college? Was it a field you found interesting or one your parents encouraged you to pursue because it fit their perception of you, the image they wanted to convey of their child, or one they believed would be lucrative? I'm not ashamed to admit I left college after two years to go directly to law school, not because I wanted to be a lawyer—I wanted to go into radio—but because my working-class Jewish parents desperately wanted their son to become a professional.

Maybe you're more independent-minded than I was, withstood parental pressure, and studied a field in which you were generally interested. In that case, how did you get your first job? Did you study various industries and companies and determine which best fit your needs and wants? Or did you take the first job you, or some contact of your professors or parents, found?

Having gotten your first job, how did you determine the path of your subsequent work life? Did you work up a long-term general plan for what you'd like to accomplish, or did you just get blown from job to job, company to company, industry to industry, based on decisions made by your superiors or personnel departments?

Finally, who's in charge of your work life today? Do you have a plan for what you'll be trying to accomplish this year, next year, and long term? Are you proactively seeking out new opportunities both at your current employer and outside the company? Or are you pinning your present and future to the decisions made by your boss and his or her boss, or to the whims of interviewers, or worse yet, résumé screeners?

Wendy Rosenfeld,[1] a willowy, auburn-haired forty-two-year-old, has never really been in charge of her work life. Despite her love of, and talent for, writing poetry, Wendy majored in journalism in college at her parents' insistence. As her father asked her once, "I don't see any want ads for poets in the paper, do you?" She landed her first job at a local newspaper thanks to the intervention of a neighbor who was a major advertiser in the publication. Because the lead reporter at the newspaper hated going to evening meetings, Wendy was given the local politics beat. After three years of covering council and board meetings, she was offered a job in the district office of the area's state senator. She took it because she wouldn't have to work nights or weekends. For the next six years she answered phones, filed, and wrote correspondence. When the state senator ran for Congress and won, he offered Wendy an equivalent job in his district office. The manager of the office left three years later and the congressman promoted Wendy to office manager. Five years later, when a job putting together the monthly mailing opened at the congressman's Washington, D.C., office, he offered it to Wendy, who accepted. But re-

1. The names and some of the details of my clients' stories throughout this book have been changed to protect their privacy.

cently, Wendy's boss decided to run for the U.S. Senate and asked Wendy to help set up his campaign headquarters back in New York. Having moved back in with her family temporarily, she came to me for help determining if she could afford to buy an apartment. After a few minutes I told her the first thing she needed to do was take charge of her own work life by developing and writing her own plan. By taking the time to plan her future, and by committing that plan to paper, Wendy would no longer find her work life governed by either her boss or fate.

## Kill Your Career . . . and Get a Job

For most of American history people didn't look to derive emotional satisfaction from their jobs. Work was to put "bread on the table." Emotional and spiritual satisfaction came from family, home, church, community, and hobbies. In the 1960s and 1970s, baby boomers rebelled against this approach. They perceived this division between financial and emotional motivations as dehumanizing. They criticized their "organization man" fathers as leading hollow lives in which they did meaningless work. In response, baby boomers created a new work concept: the career. This was a work path offering not just financial, but also emotional and spiritual, satisfaction. Boomers looked for work meaningful to them so they could lead more satisfying lives. The result, however, has been anything but.

The search for work that offers both financial and psychological satisfaction has left most people with neither. Having made such a strong commitment to their work, people today are working longer and longer hours. Meanwhile, they are spending less and less time at home, with their family, in church, in their community, or pursuing their hobbies. And despite this incredible time commitment, their income isn't secure. The pursuit of a "meaningful" career has backfired, leading baby boomers to envy the lifestyle of those gray-flannel-wearing fathers they used to criticize.

The second step in my program to win the job of your dreams is to kill your career. It may sound counterintuitive, but the best route to emotional satisfaction is stop looking for it at work. Instead, look for a job that provides as large and secure an income as possible. Look for emotional satisfaction in your personal life. If at some point in your life your need for income is reduced, you can make concessions to achieve some kind of unified "career." Until then, abandon the unhealthy notion of career and return to the far healthier concept of job.

Sean Shanahan is a forty-five-year-old graphic designer who bears a striking resemblance to the English film star Ronald Colman and who likes dressing as if he's off to a shooting weekend in the English countryside. Born and raised in Brooklyn, Sean studied at the Rhode Island School of Design. After graduating, Sean looked for work. He eschewed the advertising and publishing industries and instead looked for work with design firms. In the past two decades Sean has worked for four different design firms. He has continued to place a priority on pursuing interesting projects, despite frequently being offered "corporate" work that was better paying. Recently, Sean jumped to a start-up firm that specialized in Web design projects. But after a year the firm is still struggling. Sean is working nearly sixty hours a week. He lives alone and has little or no social life. Promised bonuses are yet to appear. Sean came in to see me to discuss rumors he has heard that one of the firm's three main clients is about to go under. Meanwhile, he received a call about a job opening at a cable television network for someone to create logos for special news and entertainment programs. It would offer him a much higher income and he wouldn't need to work as many hours. Still, he's uncertain. "I don't know if I want to be someone who creates graphics like 'Homicide in the Heartland,'" he said to me. I told him I thought homicide made sense, and it was his career he should kill.

## There's No I in Job

Most Americans have spent their lives believing there's justice in the workplace. We've been led to believe that people who show up on time and do their jobs will be safe, as long as the company can afford to keep them on. We were taught that if you show up early, stay late, and do your job well, you'll be rewarded for it, either through promotion or with pay increases. It's an accepted belief that everyone, management and staff, has the company's interests at heart, and, as a result, open and honest debate about how things should be done is encouraged and viewed positively. I'm sorry to be the one to break the news, but none of this is true.

Following the rules is no guarantee of job security. Team players get terminated as quickly as lone wolves. And excellence isn't a sure path to advancement. In fact, many bosses, threatened by excellence, will do their best to sabotage kick-ass employees. Management and coworkers usually act in their own self-interest, not in the company's interest. As a result, disagreements with your boss, however honest and well intended, lead to trouble. Most people in the workplace want to get the most reward for the least effort, want to look good more than do good, and care more about their personal success and security than the company's success and security.

Giving 110 percent and working hard for the company don't help you succeed. The secret instead is to stop focusing on your own success and worry about your boss's success instead. To paraphrase the old coaching cliché: there's no I in job. Concentrate your efforts on helping your immediate superior meet his or her goals. The more you do for your boss, the more secure your job will be, and the more you'll be rewarded. The better you make your boss look, the better you will look to him or her.

Janet Crosetti is used to dealing with double takes when people first meet her. The five-foot two-inch Korean American always responds by saying, "I know—I don't look Italian." The thirty-seven-year-old schoolteacher is married and has a six-year-old daughter named Molly. Janet worked in an urban school district when she first graduated college. Janet temporarily left the workforce to stay at home with her daughter. During that time, her husband Paul's family business boomed, enabling them to afford a home in the suburbs. When Molly started school last year, Janet decided she'd go back. An enthusiastic junior high school English teacher brimming with ideas and energy, Janet was able to land a position in a district not far from her home. While her building principal has continued to be supportive, Janet's department chairman has been giving her a hard time.

Janet and Paul came to me for some financial advice, and we then moved on to discuss her job situation. Janet told me about how she is trying to energize a department that is getting a little long in the tooth. She is constantly making suggestions, developing new and innovative lesson plans, trying to bring more multimedia into the department's offerings. But despite all her efforts, her relationship with her department chairman is getting worse. She received the first mixed evaluation of her life and was starting to worry she wouldn't get tenure in the district. I told Janet it was time for her to focus on her department chairman's needs.

## Stop Job Hunting and Go Job Fishing Instead

Believing job security would come simply from doing a good job, most people used to view job hunting as something they'd need to do only a handful of times in their lives. Everyone expected to go on a job hunt after college, but from then on it was supposed to be limited to times when there were economic or personnel upheavals beyond your control at the company. A new boss might come in and clean house to bring in his own people. Or maybe your route to promotion was permanently blocked by a peer who was promoted just above you. In any case, the job search was viewed as a reaction to circumstances.

In today's job market being terminated isn't the exception, it's the rule. Employees now are like baseball managers: they're hired to be fired. We've all become contingency workers. The constant turmoil in the job market, along with a down economy, has meant job searches are taking longer than ever. The old rule of thumb was a job search would last one month for every $10,000 you earned. Now job searches are taking two months for every $10,000. Today most people lower their expectations in order to get reemployed quicker. Since we're all now destined to be fired, and job searches take so long, it makes sense to turn job hunting into a proactive, ongoing part of your work life.

And rather than looking for the one perfect new job, you should be broadening your efforts to cultivate as many "offers" of employment as you can, which you can then either accept or reject. Instead of acting like a big-game hunter setting out on special occasions to bag a specific target, you need to act like a commercial fisherman who goes out every day and casts lots of lines in the water, checking his hooks whenever there are bites, and then deciding whether each catch is a keeper.

Jared Edwards has never had a problem making sales. Whether it was peddling photocopiers when he first graduated college, hawking woodworking equipment at state fairs, or selling music-room fixtures to schools, he was successful. But after a board shake-up led to the termination of the entire sales force at the music-fixture company, Jared had a hard time finding another sales position. His wife's salary kept the family afloat while Jared pounded the pavement, worked his network, and trolled the Internet. After six months he began taking part-time weekend and evening work as a cabinetmaker to help make ends meet. Finally, after eighteen months he landed a job selling a computerized reading-education system to school districts. When Jared and his wife came to see me it was for help cleaning up their credit, which had taken a battering during the time he was out of work. When we got around to discussing employment, Jared told me of his recent odyssey and explained how happy he was finally having a steady job. I told him not to put his job-search tools away, because he needed to start fishing for his next job right now.

## No One Hires a Stranger

In the 1980s it became conventional wisdom that "networking" was the way to get on the "inside track" to the better jobs. Networking involved making indirect approaches to individuals and asking for "advice" and "guidance." The idea was to use business contacts to get to know people who might have job openings, or who might know of job openings, which hadn't yet been advertised, and do so while avoiding the human resources department. Rather than scanning the want ads, you perused your Rolodex and schmoozed at industry gatherings to make appointments for "informational interviews." These were thinly veiled job interviews in which you did your best to impress and solicit a job offer. If none was forthcoming, you asked the person you were meeting for the name of someone else to talk to about "opportunities." Your grew your network and, inevitably, landed a new job.

This backdoor approach became institutionalized and has now become outdated and ineffective. No one falls for the "informational interview" anymore—that's why they're now so hard to come by.[2] Executives know they're simply job hunts in disguise. Human resources departments, tired of being bypassed and seeing upper-level jobs filled through networking, turned to headhunters to fill those spots. Employed executives now scrupulously avoid professional association meetings and industry gatherings because they know they'll be accosted by job hunters and overwhelmed with résumés and business cards. Of course, when these recalcitrant executives are terminated, they suddenly become regular attendees.

Instead of networking, people today need to perpetually follow a long-term track to which they add a second, short-term track if unemployed. The best long-term track today is to turn to your personal life to develop business opportunities. That's because, in my experience, no one hires a stranger anymore. With so few openings and so many candidates, people look within their own circles for candidates. It really is who you know, not what you know, that counts today. Become

---

2. I used to give one or two informational interviews a week to people sent to me by clients or associates. Now I just tell them I don't know of any jobs, but they should feel free to send a copy of their résumé for my file.

active in your church. Pursue your hobbies. Join the choir. Chat with neighbors. Attend lectures, reading groups, and city council meetings. Have as much social interaction as you can. While the odds of directly connecting with someone who has an immediate job opening isn't high in the short term, the chances of social contacts yielding job opportunities are high over the long term.

If you're unemployed you can't rely solely on long-term social activism. You also need to go back to those old-fashioned job-search options once deemed too downscale: help wanted ads and employment agencies. While these avenues may not yield the richest offerings, they do have one great advantage: they provide ready access to a stream of income. For many people who are unemployed, that's what is most needed: money coming in. Get a job . . . any job . . . and then keep looking for another job. Someone employed is always a more attractive candidate than someone unemployed.

Fred Peters is one of the most affable people you'll ever meet. A tall, distinguished-looking man, he has a wonderful sense of humor and the ability to charm most everyone he meets. An avid golfer, he's always being asked to play with new acquaintances. His wife jokes that he needs a social secretary just for his golf game. Fred's joviality has stood him in good stead in his job as director of publications for a major Ivy League university. Having to deal simultaneously with prima donna professors; penny-pinching administrators; and temperamental writers, photographers, and designers requires a great deal of patience and good humor. A recently launched round of university-wide staff cuts and consolidations has taken some of the spring out of Fred's step. He has been trying to navigate a transition of his department to a different division while keeping as much staff as possible. The unsettled nature of his situation led him to start updating his network, just in case. But he found it a daunting task. The only people who seemed to show up at the regular meetings of his professional association were out-of-work managers. His calls to business contacts and associates have rarely been returned. To top it off, the university has brought in a new president who seems intent on making another round of cuts and reorganizations. With his good humor rapidly melting, Fred called me for some advice. I told him to stop going to his professional association meetings and to play more golf instead.

## It's the Money That Counts

For the past couple of decades corporations have been greatly concerned with the "quality" of their employees' work lives. In an effort to cushion the demand for more and more time spent on the job, psychic and lifestyle rewards have become a common form of "compensation." Employers have realized that if they provide a pleasant workplace, and do things to make it easy for workers to spend more time there, they'll get less resistance to expecting fifty-hour workweeks. Provide a health club and people will show up early to work out, and will end up at their desks earlier than they otherwise would. Have a company cafeteria and people will eat in the building and either discuss work over lunch or be back at their desks sooner. Provide concierge services, like picking up prescriptions or dry cleaning, and people will work later.

All these efforts have reinforced a mistaken attitude about why we work. People have been brainwashed into thinking it's sensible to value "corporate culture" and a "supportive environment" as much as, or even more than, financial compensation. Clients often say to me:

"If I have to be at work for such a large portion of my week, it really should be a place I find appealing." Nonsense. Your focus on the job should be to increase and solidify your stream of income. Ego boosts, like a corner office, and nonfinancial rewards, like a supportive environment, are meaningless. The job of your dreams is the one that pays the most money. Today you need to accept that when it comes to a job, it's the money that counts.

Debbie O'Leary has spent more than thirty years in radio. Beginning as a deejay while in college in upstate New York, she worked her way up from doing overnights at a station in a small New England city to eventually becoming program director at the number one station in a midsized midwestern city. Through it all she worked only at rock stations, since it was her love of rock music that got her into radio in the first place. It was love that brought her to New York as well. She met her husband, Bruce Warshaw, at a radio convention. Unlike Debbie, Bruce had spent his entire radio career in the New York market, working his way up to an afternoon drive-time shift at one of the city's premier rock stations. Debbie, who was born in the New York suburbs and still had family there, moved back to New York and married Bruce. Getting a job in the crowded, competitive New York radio market was tough for Debbie. After looking for work for more than eighteen months she received two offers: a low-paying part-time replacement deejay position at one of the city's rock stations, and a higher-paying job as jazz programmer at a satellite radio network. Debbie jokingly said she'd have to be deaf in order to deal with the jazz job. I suggested she buy some earplugs because it's the money that counts.

## Hello, I Must Be Going

The first day on a new job is both frightening and exciting. Part of you is worried, unsure how you'll be received or what the company is really like. Another part of you is eager, hoping the job will live up to all your hopes and dreams. The last thing you're apt to consider on your first day is how you'll be leaving. Yet that's exactly what you should be thinking.

In an environment in which there's no job security at all, and job tenure is shrinking yearly, it's essential to go into every new job with your eyes wide open. You *will* be leaving this job. No one works for the same company for his or her entire work life anymore. In fact, almost no one works for the same company for even a decade anymore. Either you'll find a better-paying job and leave of your own accord, or you will be terminated. There is no third result.

Because your departure is certain, it's vital that you plan for it from day one, or even earlier. What would make you leave this job? What negative developments would force you to jump ship? What positive attributes of another job would lead you to grab it? If possible, you can even try to negotiate the terms of your departure by getting a full-blown employment contract or a simple termination agreement.

Bill Kaplan was ecstatic to be finally graduating college. A very bright, creative young man, he had a checkered and peripatetic college career. He began as a fine-arts major at a small private college, but transferred to a state university after a year and changed his major to theater arts. After a year he dropped out, moved to New York City, took waiter jobs, and tried to line up acting work. After two unsuccessful years he went back to school at a city university as an English major

22

and finally graduated. Fascinated by the bookstore business, Bill was thrilled to line up a job as a management trainee at a large chain bookstore not far from where he went to college. He came to see me for a life-planning session, which was a graduation gift from his sister. After hearing him wax enthusiastic about his new job I said I hated to rain on his opening day but it was time to figure out why and when he'd be leaving.

## The Returns on Your Investment

There's no denying following these seven steps will require you to make an investment of time and energy. And I also realize that asking you to buy into some of my unconventional ideas will require you to make a leap of faith. Believe me, you won't regret it. The returns on your investments of time, energy, and faith will be incredible. Throughout this book I'll be describing how this approach to work has turned the lives of my clients around. But for now let me quickly run down the potential benefits.

Fire your boss and you'll be in control of your work life. You'll never end up like Wendy Rosenfeld, leading a reactive work life, blown here and there by fate and happenstance. She followed my program, drafted a career plan, and took back control of her life.

Fire your boss and you'll find the emotional and psychological satisfaction you've always sought but never found. You'll stop being like Sean Shanahan, working longer and longer hours and getting less and less satisfaction. Sean listened to me, killed his career, and ended up happier than he imagined possible.

Fire your boss and you'll have job security. Rather than being at the mercy of your boss, like Janet Crosetti, you'll find your position safer than ever. Janet started focusing on her boss's needs, rather than her own, and cemented her position.

Fire your boss and you'll never find yourself desperately looking for work. You won't end up like Jared Edwards, constantly having to scrounge for a job to keep food on the table. Jared followed my advice and began job fishing, and as a result, has always had a new job on the line.

Fire your boss and you won't need to go through an extended job search. Fred Peters found his network had dried up and the classified ads were barren, until he accepted that no one hires a stranger today. By tapping into his personal life he finally found job opportunities.

Fire your boss and you'll be able to maintain and grow your income. Rather than accepting pay cuts and lower salaries, as did Debbie O'Leary, you'll be able to maximize your earnings. She took my advice and decided it's the money that counts. Since then her income has grown at a steady rate.

Fire your boss and you'll never be fired. Instead of waiting for the inevitable ax to fall, you'll always be able to leave on your own terms, at the most advantageous time. Bill Kaplan eventually followed my advice and was able to "quit" his way into one better job after another.

## Four Quick Inducements

Having preached contrarian solutions to problems in the past, I know they can be hard for some people to accept.[3] I realize it's asking a lot for you to suddenly drop the job attitudes you've been taught by all

3. As the author of *Die Broke*, which encourages people to use their assets to the fullest extent possible during their lives and forgo leaving an estate, I'm used to getting some resistance.

your previous mentors and advisers and adopt a revolutionary approach preached by someone you've never met, no matter how rosy a picture I've painted of the potential benefits. So let me offer you four quick inducements to at least continue on reading.

First, as you'll see by the stories of my clients' successes, this approach is working well for people now—even in what is one of the worst job markets in the nation. The essential elements of this approach, as outlined in the seven steps, are applicable to everyone in America, regardless of where he or she lives.

Second, what have you got to lose by considering my approach? Those of you who have been out of work for some time already know the traditional approach isn't working. Trying to get a new job today using yesterday's techniques is like trying to tunnel through a brick wall with a spoon. It is possible, but it is incredibly difficult and could take years. Why not give my approach a chance? If you're unhappy with it you can always return to the spoon. Those of you who are still employed have the luxury of investing in new ideas before you need them. Again, if you're not convinced by what I write, you can stick with the traditional ideas—just make sure your boss hasn't seen you reading this book.

Third, this is the perfect time to adopt a new approach to the workplace. It has become a cliché to say we're living in a transitional time. However, despite its becoming a hackneyed observation, it remains true. The workplace has clearly changed. Yet, the widely accepted approaches to finding and thriving on the job have not. Most people are still following the old patterns. This allows those who adopt new patterns to really stand out from the crowd. Think of it as getting in on the ground floor. I'm not saying everyone will be following my approach in the future. But clearly they will be following some new approach. Those who abandon the old, outmoded techniques first will be in the best position for the future.

And fourth, I believe my approach offers an unprecedented opportunity not only to increase the size and security of your stream of income, but also to increase your chances of getting the emotional satisfaction so many of us currently lack. Increase your income. Make your job more secure. Find psychological satisfaction. All this is possible in today's job market, as long as you're willing to at least temporarily unlock any airtight compartments in your mind and consider some new ideas. Turn the page to break the seal and let in some fresh air.

# CHAPTER 2

# Fire Your Boss . . . and Hire Yourself

*In every one of those little stucco boxes there's some poor bastard who's never free except when he's fast asleep and dreaming he's got the boss down the bottom of a well and is bunging lumps of coal at him.*

—GEORGE ORWELL

ALL NATHAN WINKLE'S friends and coworkers think he's a control freak. Nathan's clothes closet looks like a display in a men's store. His files at work are perfectly alphabetized, using color-coded labels and tricut folders in pristine order. He tracks his auto mileage and brings his car in for an oil change as soon as it has been driven three thousand miles. Nathan follows his investments online daily, and prepares his taxes on January 1. The tools in his garage are mounted on Peg-Boards. His wife jokes that she and the kids don't stand still long for fear Nathan will use his labeling machine to label them on their foreheads. Yet despite his being a control freak, Nathan had his territory at work changed twice in the last year. Nathan's boss had him change his vacation plans twice, to accommodate the boss's changing plans. There were dozens of other things that all added up to Nathan's feeling as if he had no control of his work life. It was as if he were a marionette, with his somewhat flaky boss holding the strings. But in the past year Nathan has changed all that. He decided when to take his vacation this year . . . and his boss rearranged his own schedule to accommodate him. Nathan was able to pick and choose which projects he worked on, which trade shows were worth attending, for how long, and where he would stay. His secret? He adopted the first element in my workplace philosophy: he fired his boss and hired himself. You should do the same.

Americans are obsessed with taking charge . . . except when it comes to their work lives.

I know people who obsessively take charge of their gardens, selecting where to place different perennials to ensure the colors and heights don't clash and there's a constant supply of blooms during spring and summer.

Lots of parents today take charge of their child's life, scheduling everything from sports to study. Some go so far as to plan out a complex social, cultural, and academic pattern to get the child into not just the right college, but the right preschool.

Professions to help us take charge of our lives abound. There are professional tax planners, estate planners, investment planners, kitchen planners, landscape planners, even party planners.

Yet when it comes to work, the element of our life that provides the fuel (money) for so much else, and that occupies so much of our time, we cede control to others.[4]

---

4. Sure, there are lots of people who play office politics and who try to maneuver their way through an organization's bureaucracy or up a corporate ladder. I'll get into those efforts later in this book, but I don't characterize them as taking charge. That kind of activity is tactical; it's short-term and reactive. Taking charge of your own work life means being strategic; it's long-term and proactive.

Most of us have almost no control over our work lives. Our boss has the power to fire us at will, for no reason. In effect, every supervisor, every employer, is potentially a miniature George Steinbrenner, able to terminate impulsively if he or she so wishes. But the power to terminate isn't the only weapon the boss has in his or her arsenal. The boss decides when you should arrive and when you can depart. The boss chooses where you sit and when you can go to lunch. The boss sets dress codes. The boss must approve the timing of your vacation. The boss determines your responsibilities and obligations, and how long you have to meet them. The boss dictates how you are supposed to do your job, and what tools you are allowed to use. The boss judges whether your work is acceptable or not, and whether you deserve an increase in compensation.

Think I'm overstating the case? Let's see. Take out a notebook or pad and a pen or pencil. If there aren't many blank pages left, go out and buy a new one. I'm going to be asking you to do exercises throughout this book, so you'll be needing it often. Ask yourself these questions and write down your answers.

1. What is your value in the workplace?

2. What kinds of benefits do you deserve?

3. What skills do you have?

4. What do you consider your greatest achievements?

5. How long do you think you need to work at a particular job or task to master it and be ready to move on to another job or task?

6. Do you have a personal plan for your work life?

Let's go over your answers one by one.

## 1. What Is Your Value in the Workplace?

Okay, I'll bet you wrote down your salary or something close to it. Now let me ask you another question. Why do you assume your current salary indicates your value in the workplace? Odds are you've no independent assessment of that. Instead, you're depending on your boss for an estimate of your value. If you're like most of us, you accepted the initial salary offered by your first employer. Subsequently you've expressed thanks for every raise you've been granted and understanding for every increase that's been delayed or denied. After all, what can you do about it? A lot actually, as you'll soon see.

## 2. What Kinds of Benefits Do You Deserve?

Once again, I'll wager that the benefits you listed are those you're currently receiving. When you were told that the company needed to shift to an HMO or that your copayment had to be increased, you were annoyed, right? But you assumed you've no control over the situation, and that the benefit was industry-wide practice, didn't you? You've let your boss determine what you deserve.

## 3. What Skills Do You Have?

I'll bet you've listed a package of skills that were assembled based on what your employer wanted you to do. If the company believed someone in your position should be able to create a database, you were told to learn how. If the company said your job description required you to write press releases, someone taught you how. Most of us have developed a bundle of talents based on our employer's needs rather than our own. If you've been on the job for a while, you've put together the perfect package . . . for this job at this company.

## 4. What Do You Consider Your Greatest Achievements?

Take a look at your list and note if you personally value any of these achievements. If you're lucky, maybe one or two of your achievements resonate with you personally. That's because most of us have let our employers dictate what type of achievements are valued. In a company with little regard for customer service but that places a priority on customer turnover and traffic, you may be rewarded for keeping your interactions with customers short rather than polite. Perhaps you work for a firm that values quality over profitability. While specifically tailoring your achievements to your company is a good way to ingratiate yourself with your boss—something I'll talk a great deal about later in this book—it can narrow your horizons.

## 5. How Long Do You Think You Need to Work at a Particular Job or Task to Master It and Be Ready to Move On to Another Job or Task?

Okay, where did you come up with this number? Is your assessment based on objective criteria, or does it come from your boss telling you "you're not ready" or because there's a company "icon" frozen in place above you in the hierarchy?

## 6. Do You Have a Personal Plan for Your Work Life?

Have most of the stops in your career followed a well-thought-out plan that you developed with the help of some unbiased mentors and advisers? Or have you gone from position to position and/or job to job because of the whims and needs of your boss or the twists of fate? Other than those who have become entrepreneurs, every one of my clients, from the wealthy, Ivy League–educated corporate executive to the struggling immigrant cab driver, has progressed through his or her work life without a personal work plan.

## The Ultimate Weapon Is Ultimately Powerless

When I first point out to clients how little control they have over their work lives, their response is usually something like this: "Well, I still have the ultimate power; I can quit."

Granted, since slavery and indentured servitude have been outlawed in America, we all now have what most people perceive to be the ultimate doomsday workplace weapon: the power to walk out anytime you want. Having this power may make you feel better—"I'll show him . . . I'll quit!"—but that's about all it can do. And the palliative effect is pretty short term. Quitting impulsively (as opposed to giving notice) stops feeling good just about the time you're leaving the building. Having the power to quit is the equivalent of having the power to commit workplace suicide.

Quitting isn't an effective power, since you can be replaced. Don't get me wrong. I'm sure you're incredibly good at what you do. And I'm certain if you walked away from your job tomorrow the office would be in a state of turmoil. But not for long.

No one is indispensable. I don't care how loyal your customers are to you personally, or that you're the only one who knows how the accounts-payable system works. FDR died while the United States was still fighting World War II, leaving the presidency in the hands of Harry S. Truman, who had been vice president for less than a year and hadn't been brought into the decision-making process, and whose only executive experience was running a men's clothing store into the ground. The war effort didn't skip a beat. Everyone can be replaced.

When you quit you hurt yourself and your former coworkers. Your boss won't be staying late to clean up the mess—unless he or she is the only other person who works for the company. The burden will fall to your former coworkers.

## Past Efforts to Balance the Power Have Failed

That's one reason why the pioneers of workers' rights in America, and around the world, decided to organize labor into unions. If all the workers in the company stuck together, the boss would have to replace everyone at the same time. And if workers in separate companies throughout an industry supported each other, it could really put the squeeze on employers. Having effectively organized, the labor movement was able to use its power politically as well. Politicians, eager to gain the support of labor, helped enact laws that protected workers from some of the worst practices of employers.

Similarly, the civil rights movement and the women's movement led to legislation that protected employees against discriminatory practices. Beginning with laws protecting employees against racial discrimination, the umbrella of protective legislation has expanded to cover religious and ethnic minorities, women, older Americans, homosexuals, and the disabled. (See the box on page 34: How Protected Are You?)

## HOW PROTECTED ARE YOU?

There are a number of different federal, state, and local laws that protect people against discrimination in the workplace. How protected you are depends on a great number of factors, including your age, ethnic background, health, and where you live.

Everyone in the United States is potentially protected by federal legislation. There's Title VII of the Civil Rights Act of 1964, which prohibits job bias on the basis of race, color, sex, religion, and national origin. Then there's the Age Discrimination in Employment Act, which prohibits job bias against individuals forty years of age and over. There's also the Americans with Disabilities Act, which prohibits job bias against individuals with disabilities who work for employers with fifteen or more employees. Finally, there's Section 510 of the Employee Retirement Income Security Act, which prohibits discrimination against an individual in connection with his or her entitlement to pension benefits.

You may have additional protection depending on where you live, since states, and some cities, have their own laws offering workplace protection, often expanding the federal protections dramatically. For example, New York State Human Rights Law prohibits job bias on the basis of age (eighteen and over), race, creed, color, national origin, disability, sex, or marital status. New York City law goes on to prohibit discrimination against someone because of his or her own actual or perceived age, creed, color, national origin, disability, sexual orientation, or alienage or citizenship status, as well as the actual or perceived age, creed, color, national origin, disability, sexual orientation, or alienage or citizenship status of someone with whom he or she has a known relationship or association. Contact either your state department of labor or your local state legislator's office to find out what state or city protections you may have. Of course, remember that the best protection you can have is to assume control of your own work life.

All these noble efforts to redress the imbalance of power in the workplace haven't really had a major impact. Sure, if you are singled out and terminated because of your race, national origin, age, gender, disability, or sexual orientation, you can successfully win a legal judgment. However, you can be a blind sixty-year-old African American lesbian bookkeeper from France, and if you're just one of a hundred other people let go because the company decided to outsource all the back-office functions, you don't have a case. And don't expect much solidarity either.

The American labor movement's rise to power was tied to the rise of manufacturing as the driving force in the American economy. As manufacturing has declined, so has the strength of the labor movement. With a few notable exceptions (teachers, professional athletes), the labor movement hasn't been able to successfully organize information or service-industry workers. No one has been able to convince the twenty-four-year-old single mother working at a day-care center, the thirty-five-year-old college graduate writing code for a software company, and the forty-five-year-old account executive at an advertising agency that they have any common cause with the auto worker, or with each other, for that matter. We've become a nation of rugged individualist workers and "intrapreneurs." That's been great for corporate productivity and profitability but, as it turns out, not so great for individual security and fulfillment. In this environment the only way for you to take control of your work life and create the job of your dreams is to fire your boss and hire yourself.

## The Answer: Take Charge

I'm not suggesting you walk into your boss's office tomorrow and announce you're staging a coup d'état. You might as well announce you're quitting—and we've already seen how ineffective that is. Firing your boss and hiring yourself as manager of your own work life is primarily a mental exercise. Like many of the steps I'll be outlining in this book, it's an attitude adjustment, a different way of looking at your work life, which will change the way you think and act in the future.

Outwardly, even though you've fired your boss, you will still appear as loyal or subservient as ever. In fact, if you follow the rest of the steps in this book, you'll seem even more dedicated to your boss than before. On the inside, however, you'll be the one pulling the strings. You'll be the one determining your value in the workplace and deciding the kind of benefits you deserve. You'll be the one selecting the skills you should add to your repertoire. You'll be the one setting goals and measuring your success. And you'll be the one deciding when you're ready to move on to another job or task, because you'll have a personal work plan.

That may sound very complicated. It's really not. You need to go through a four-step process of self-examination and exploration. Get out your pad or notebook again. Label one page Job Description, a second Performance Review, a third Alternate Paths, and a fourth Work Plan.

## 1. Write Your Own Job Description

On the top of the first page, write a brief description of your job.

Now, let's consider what you've written. Most people write the equivalent of a want ad. While that's probably an accurate outline of what you do at work, there's a problem with viewing the specifics of your current responsibilities as your job description.

When you embrace such a description you're surrendering control of your own work identity, either to your boss or to the conventions of your profession.

Those who are most traditional probably see themselves first as a company man or woman. They might write, as one of my clients, Jenny Moreno, did when I first began working with her: "I work for Acme Computer as a technical writer preparing software manuals."

Others who have soured on company identification may define themselves by profession or specialization. They might write, as another client of mine, Paul Derschinsky, did after witnessing some layoffs: "I'm a photographer currently working for the *Gotham Daily Bugle* on the breaking news beat."

While both descriptions may be factually correct, they're emblematic of giving up control. By identifying yourself by company allegiance you're letting the firm define you. By identifying yourself by profession or specialization you're letting an industry or discipline define you. To take charge of your work life you need to define yourself instead. A self-created job description lets you set the framework for how the work world will perceive you. This will expand the jobs you're qualified to fill.

Go back to that page on which you wrote your initial job description. To develop your own definition you first need to dig down into the details. What do you do each day, each week, and each month? Don't reflexively write your answers. Think about the question a minute, and then try to describe your activities in as generalized a way as you can, eliminating jargon and terminology tied to your company, industry, or profession. Focus on the verbs you use in your description, the words that describe activity.

Let's return to Jenny Moreno. I worked with her on breaking down what it was she actually did, in order to develop her own job description. When a new software application was developed, Jenny was given a large, very technical report created by its designers, which explained what it did, and how it worked. She was also given a sample of the application to explore and test, and a description of the target end user. Jenny first digested the technical report. Second, she studied the sample product itself. Third, she analyzed the needs and wants of the intended end user. Jenny then finished by preparing a manuscript that put the product's features and capabilities into a form that made it comprehensible and useful to the end user. Jenny and I then worked on getting past the language and terminology of the computer business. After focusing on the verbs she used, we came up with the following job description: "I gather, analyze, and digest complex information and then translate and present it in a form that meets the needs of a particular audience."

Go through your notes on your activities, removing jargon, and focusing on the verbs. Refine the language as much as possible, the goal being reducing it to a single sentence. Now, rewrite this sentence in **ALL CAPITAL LETTERS** at the bottom of the page you labeled Job Description.

## 2. Give Yourself a Performance Review

When you're not in charge of your work life, all the parameters by which you're measured and then rewarded, in both the present and the future, are determined by your boss. What are you paid? Your boss decides what the pay range should be for your position, and whether or not you're worthy of a salary in the upper part of the range. Your boss sets the standards by which you'll be measured to see whether or not you qualify for an increase. The skills you acquire and hone, the achievements you strive for, and the pace with which you progress are all based on your boss's decisions.

As long as you work for this person, you'll need to make sure you take his or her decisions into account. But if that's all you do, you'll find it's hard to move into the job of your dreams. Just as you need to develop your own job description, you need also to conduct your own performance review.

Start by becoming an expert, not just on your company or your industry, but on the job market in general. Using your new, self-created job description, research what other individuals who fit that description earn in salary and benefits. That means expanding your reading of the classified ads, perhaps by checking business journals at your local library, and spending some time searching for salary surveys on the Internet. While you're at it, contact your college's career office and see if the counselors there can provide any comparative information. In addition to noting compensation packages, pay attention to the skills that are stressed in these other fields. What achievements seem to be valued? How much and what type of past experience do these other fields require? Take notes on your findings, writing them on the page you've labeled Performance Review.

Paul Derschinsky, my news photographer client, went through this exercise recently. Rather than just looking at how much other photographers at his newspaper, or news photographers in general, were paid, Paul started researching the salary and benefit packages of magazine photographers, photography teachers, camera-store managers, corporate photographers, and even photographers who worked for the government. He spent one Saturday in the reference room of a university library near his home, and the next day doing online research at home. Paul discovered that while his salary was about average for a newspaper or magazine photographer with his skills and experience, it was a bit higher than the salary of a product manager for a photo-equipment company, a camera-store manager, or a photography teacher. But corporate and wedding photographers earned more, and seemed to require less experience to move up to more lucrative positions. For obvious reasons, those hiring and assessing corporate and wedding photographers placed more emphasis on portrait and studio work than those employing news photographers. Paul determined that while newspaper photography was perhaps more exciting than corporate and wedding work, it paid less and offered a slower climb up the salary ladder. He also learned that the skills he was developing and refining, his candid photography and expertise in digital-image transfer, weren't valued highly in corporate or wedding work. In those fields, studio work was more important, and electronic editing was prized. He made notes of his findings.

## 3. Define Alternate Courses

By developing your own job description and conducting a performance self-evaluation, you're almost guaranteed to discover that there are alternate courses open to you today and in the future. That's one of the great side benefits of firing your boss and hiring yourself: suddenly your work horizons are much broader.

Turn back to the page with your new job description. Read it over to yourself and brainstorm about all the fields and occupations that would fit this general description. Don't worry about being realistic. Give your imagination free rein. Ask your family and friends for their input too. Write down all your ideas on the page you've labeled Alternate Paths.

Jenny Moreno, reading over her new job description, realized she wasn't qualified to be only a technical writer for a computer software company. She could be a speechwriter for a politician, an analyst for the CIA, an author of how-to books, a journalist for a consumer publication, or a report writer for a think tank or foundation.

Similarly, Paul Derschinsky realized he didn't need to be a news photographer. He could become a corporate photographer, a wedding photographer, or a magazine photographer; or he could teach photography, manage a camera store, or go to work for a company that manufactures photo equipment.

## 4. Put Your Plan in Writing

Self-redefinition and self–performance review do more than just expand your short-term job horizons. They free you psychologically and emotionally from the narrow work path you may have been traveling. You're no longer forced to follow the predetermined pattern created by your boss or your profession. You can now develop your own plan for your work life, which ensures that your future steps help you keep all the alternate courses you've uncovered open, rather than close them off.

Odds are you've found you need to acquire new skills or pursue different achievements to improve your chances to land other jobs. Give some thought to how you can do that. Just make sure you don't do anything to risk your standing at your current job. That's not as tough as it sounds at first. Most often you won't find outright conflict between your efforts to secure your current job and prepare for your next job. Instead, it's usually a matter of developing what I've always called "bifocal vision": focusing on your current job and your future job at the same time. If you're having trouble coming up with ideas, speak with family, friends, mentors, career counselors, even clergy. Anyone with an open mind can be helpful. Write your thoughts and findings down on the page you've labeled Work Plan.

> For Paul, the realization that he could make more money, faster, in the corporate or wedding world wasn't so much a shock as a wake-up call. He'd known that news photographers literally paid a price for the excitement and glamour of their jobs. He just hadn't known how high that price was. While he isn't yet convinced he wants to make the jump to the corporate world, he is taking steps to ensure he could. After a conversation with one of his favorite college professors, who had remained a mentor, he came up with a plan. He has signed up for a graduate class in electronic imaging and a masters seminar in portrait work. An added bonus is that these courses will put him on a path to get his master's degree, which will help if he wants to become a photography teacher.

Over the more than twenty years I've been coaching people, I've learned that recording your ideas and plans on paper is essential. Writing everything down not only offers a chance to refine your thoughts, but also gives you a map you'll be able to refer to in the future. Whenever I counsel entrepreneurs, I tell them their business plan is vital, not just because it helps focus thinking and efforts, but because it provides a blueprint for future success and failure. The same is true for putting your own work plan in writing. For instance, by noting the skills and achievements you need to remain a viable candidate for alternate paths, as well as the ways you're planning to acquire those skills and achievements, you can continually refer back to them, to ensure you're still on course and your chosen techniques are working.

The final form your written work plan takes is entirely up to you. It can remain just the page on which you've recorded your thoughts and ideas. Or it could be handwritten in a small notebook you carry about, or recorded as a word-processing document, or as an outline on your laptop or PDA. Paul, for example, kept his work plan as a word-processing document on his laptop computer. Jenny, on the other hand, handwrote a "mission statement," and kept it on her refrigerator at home so she could see it every morning. The most important thing is that your plan spells out your self-definition, the alternate paths available to you, the skills you need to add, and the way you intend to add them, all in a form to which you can repeatedly refer.

## Wendy Rosenfeld Fires Her Boss and Hires Herself

If you remember back to chapter 1, Wendy Rosenfeld had come to see me about buying an apartment. When she told me how her work life had involved repeated job changes and moves based on the needs of her boss, a politician, I told her she needed to fire the congressman and elect herself as boss of her work life.

Wendy began by developing her own job description. Although in the course of her work Wendy had done everything from answering letters to managing an office, she realized that her most recent role had been her most valuable: putting together the congressman's monthly mailing to constituents. She and I worked on developing a general description of exactly what that involved. After removing the jargon and focusing on the verbs, we came up with this: "I gather,

---

### WENDY ROSENFELD'S WORK PLAN

JOB DESCRIPTION:
- I gather, compile, and present information of interest to a specific audience in an attractive package that also presents my client or employer in the best possible light.

POTENTIAL ALTERNATE ROLES:
1. Editor/writer of constituent newsletters
2. Editor/writer of promotional brochures for companies or organizations
3. Editor/writer of annual reports
4. Editor/writer of sales and marketing materials for manufacturers

PERFORMANCE REVIEW:
1. Earning market-value pay for editor of constituent newsletters

---

compile, and present information of interest to a specific audience in an attractive package that also presents my client or employer in the best possible light."

Wendy and I then brainstormed about other roles that fit her self-generated description. She also spoke with her sister. Together we decided that besides putting together constituent newsletters, Wendy could prepare promotional brochures for companies or organizations, put together annual reports, or develop sales materials for manufacturers.

Next, Wendy gave herself a performance review. Some quick informal research on Capitol Hill showed her that she was earning

2. Earning more than market value for editor of materials for not-for-profits

3. Earning less than market value for any of the other alternate paths

4. Need to improve graphics skills for better-paying paths

### ALTERNATE COURSES:

1. For greater stability, work in development for not-for-profit agencies or organizations.

2. For greater income and quicker advancement, work in corporate communications.

### ACTIONS:

1. Take night class at community college to learn page layout/Web design programs.

2. Investigate graphic design courses.

about the same amount as the other congressional staffers who put together constituent mailings, and that her career had progressed at a comparable rate. However, a quick visit to the career office at her alma mater showed her that she was earning less than she would if she were putting together almost any other kind of promotional material, whether brochures, annual reports, or sales materials. All of those areas would also offer a quicker pace of salary advancement. The only way she would be paid less or be on a slower track was if she were preparing fund-raising materials for not-for-profit agencies or organizations. Those other areas put more emphasis on the ability to use more sophisticated graphics.

Wendy then defined her alternate courses. She realized she could earn more, quicker, by working in corporate communications. Alternatively, she could work in development for not-for-profit agencies or organizations and have greater stability than in politics or in corporate communications. Wendy decided to take a night class at a community college to learn a page-layout program and investigated taking some graphic-design courses in order to add the skills she needed to keep both her options open.

Finally, Wendy put her work plan in writing by preparing an outline on her computer, noting her job description, the alternate paths open to her, the skills she needed to add, and how she planned to go about acquiring them. She printed out the outline and hung it over her desk at home. (See the box on page 44: Wendy Rosenfeld's Work Plan.) When she brought me a copy of her outline, I congratulated her on firing her boss.

If you've followed the steps I've outlined in this chapter, you deserve my congratulations as well. If you do nothing else I talk about in this book other than this first step, you've nonetheless made tremendous progress. By firing your boss and hiring yourself instead, you've done what most Americans dream of but don't believe possible: you've taken control of your work life. From now on, you will be the one who determines your work future. That's nothing to sneeze at. But to go on and lead the life of your dreams you need to take the next step: kill your career. If you're ready to seize your own happiness, move on to chapter 3.

# Kill Your Career . . . and Get a Job

*The word career is a divisive word. It's a word that divides the normal life from business or professional life.*

—GRACE PALEY

MARK TAPLEY IS no longer depressed. For years he had felt that he was living a catch-22. Having grown up in a very poor home with an absentee father, he was determined to provide the kind of life for his children that he himself hadn't experienced. An accountant, Mark labored at his profession, moving up to partner in a large firm and earning enough to buy a lovely sprawling home with a pool for his family. He could send his kids to the best private schools and summer camps. Unfortunately, he was a stranger to them. Mark was spending so much time at the office to provide for his children that he was depriving them of a father in the process. It was a cycle he couldn't figure out how to break . . . until this past year. Now he's home for dinner every night and spends every weekend with the family. He and his wife have had to cut back on the summer camps, but now they're all going away together for two weeks in the summer. All it took for Mark to break the cycle was for him to take the second step in my workplace philosophy: he killed his career and got a job instead. It will work for you as well.

There is a way to get more satisfaction from life.

You can make a difference in the world.

It's possible to achieve the personal and spiritual fulfillment you've always wanted.

Ironically, it's by giving up the notion of career that you'll actually accomplish the goal that careers were created to meet.

The period from the end of World War II until the mid-1960s was an age of both prosperity and conformity. Whether he actually wore a gray flannel suit or went to work in overalls, and whether he lived in the city, the country, or the rapidly growing suburbs, your father probably strived to put physical as well as emotional distance between himself and his work. That was certainly true for the father of Sean Shanahan, the graphic designer I wrote of back in chapter 1.

## Rebelling Against a Divided Life

Sean's father saw his home as a refuge from his job with the telephone company and signaled, both verbally and nonverbally, that he really didn't want to talk about work once he came home. Sean's mom was a full-time homemaker who really did turn their house in Brooklyn into a sanctuary and refuge. For Sean's parents there was a sharp divide between work life and personal life.

If you're like most of my clients, you grew up, like Sean, seeing the downside to this divided life. Perhaps your dad seemed not to like what he did for a living. Sean believed his father was unhappy working as an executive with the telephone company. Maybe you sensed your mom had ambitions that weren't fulfilled. Sean believed his mother would have gone to nursing school had she not started a family so young. Most of my clients consciously set out to be different from their parents. Whether male or female, they—and probably you—went looking for meaningful work, work that was satisfying, work that made a difference.

Instead of getting a job—which was what your dad called work— I'll bet you looked for a career. Instead of feeling you had to choose between fulfilling parenthood and fulfilling work, you probably decided you could have both. Instead of work being a means to an end, you wanted it to become an end in itself. By taking a different approach than your parents, you believed, you would lead a more emotionally, psychologically, and spiritually rewarding life. That was what Sean believed. For most of his working life, he assiduously chose "art over commerce," as he put it, trying to reap psychological rather than material rewards.

However, that's not the way things worked out for him, nor for most of my clients. Maybe, like them, you succeeded in avoiding the sharply divided life of your parents. But unfortunately, if your experience was anything like my clients' experiences, it turned out to be a life that was mostly work. Because you were pursuing something "meaningful" or something you found "rewarding," you tended to spend most of your day at work. Nine to five, five days a week is for those who are punching a clock, you thought. You have a calling, and so you're at the office from eight to eight, and you bring work home on the weekend too. Besides, there's now the not-so-subtle pressure from your boss to stay on the job until your work (and the work of the two people who were laid off) is done.

When you are home, in an effort to make the most of your limited time together you schedule "quality" family events. You, your partner, and maybe even your children coordinate schedules via cell phone during the day, instantly compensating for late meetings at the office or impromptu playdates after school. On the weekend your life is a whirlwind of home repairs, chauffeuring kids, and taking care of the things you didn't have the time for during the week.

What's really troubling, however, isn't that you're so tired or that your life is so hectic. The real trouble is that your work isn't as satisfying as it should be. It's certainly not rewarding enough to justify the sacrifices you're making in your personal life.

Sean's dad had a job that might not have been "meaningful," but he was home for dinner with the family every night and could spend Sunday afternoon playing catch with the kids. His mom might have had to let go of some of her ambitions, but she was able to pick her children up after school every day and make a big family dinner on Sundays. Sean feels he has no personal life to speak of. He finds himself working even longer hours, isn't earning as much as he believes he should, and has no job security. Earlier this year Sean confessed to me, "I'll never be Ward Cleaver, but I do envy some of the lifestyle of my parents." I told him he wasn't the only one.

## A Divided Life Isn't So Bad After All

Don't get me wrong. I'm not calling for a return to the *Leave It to Beaver* lifestyle . . . unless that's what you want. Instead, I'm suggesting you take a different approach to work, one that offers a better chance of getting both the financial and psychological rewards you've wanted. What's that approach? I'm suggesting you stop living to work and instead start working to live. Rather than looking at work as an end in itself, view it as a means to an end: a way to generate the money you need to have a happy life. It's time to kill your career and get a job instead. (See the box on page 51: Definitions and Earliest Known Use.)

---

## DEFINITIONS AND EARLIEST KNOWN USE

According to the *Oxford English Dictionary:*

JOB

**2.** A piece of work, or transaction, done for hire, or with a special view to profit. **1660** Pepys, *Diary:* I will do all the good jobs I can.

CAREER

**5.** A person's course or progress through life (or a distinct portion of life), especially when publicly conspicuous, or abounding in remarkable incidents; similarly with reference to a nation, a political party, etc. **b.** In modern language frequently used for: A course of professional life or employment, which affords opportunity for progress or advancement in the world. **1803** Wellington, *Dispatches:* A more difficult negotiation than you ever had in your diplomatic career.

---

Once you start looking at work as first and foremost a moneymaking endeavor, you'll find you actually start making more money. I'll talk more about this approach in a later chapter, but for now let me just say that killing your career almost guarantees a larger income, since from now on, whenever you face a choice or decision, you'll always opt for the path that provides more money.

But let's put the money issue aside for a few chapters. Right now let's focus on satisfaction. After all, if you're like most of my clients, you didn't pursue a career to earn more money; you wanted fulfillment. The problem is that in your pursuit of fulfillment through work you've stolen time from the areas of life that are far more likely to provide fulfillment: personal relationships, community, hobbies, and religion.

Instead of looking to better society through your work, why not do it after work? Sure, it's possible to find a job that directly or indirectly helps the poor. That would indeed be a noble pursuit. But if that's your goal, why not volunteer at a soup kitchen instead? That's far easier to achieve and guaranteed to offer the kind of rewards you're seeking.

Looking for creative fulfillment? There are people who are able to find work that provides artistic satisfaction, but they are few and far between. Instead, why not paint watercolors on the weekend? You'll be creating what you want, not what someone else demands.

Rather than working hour after hour at a job you hope will give you a sense of emotional satisfaction, spend more time at home with your life partner and children and family and friends. You're far more likely to get emotional satisfaction from teaching your daughter to ride a two-wheeler than from making a killer presentation to the board.

Crave a sense of community? Get active in your house of worship or a local service organization. Being a member of a congregation, for instance, is more likely to give you a sense of belonging than being named to the project team for the Acme account.

Sometimes, when I suggest to clients that they kill their career, I'm met with indignation. Clients ask if I'm saying they can't have it all, that it's a mistake to look for work in a field they love, or that it's impossible to find satisfaction at work today. I've thought a great deal about that question because it's a fair one and deserves an honest, thoughtful answer.

## "Can't I Have It All?"

Is it possible to have it all? To have a job you love that is both rewarding and lucrative, as well as a satisfying personal life? I will admit it is possible. But, truth be told, it's not probable. It's a one-in-a-million chance. A real long shot. How many social workers or poets earn six figures? How many executives pulling down seven-figure salaries are home every night for dinner with their family? Sure, there are some, but I see them as the exceptions that prove the rule.

And look at what you'd be risking in the gamble to be one of these few. You'd be giving up surefire opportunities to achieve some of your cherished goals on a roll of the dice to try to achieve all of them. I'm not willing to take that risk with your life. Instead, I'd rather help you kill your career.

Let me tell you a little story that perhaps will illustrate my point. It's a well-known fable that comes in various incarnations. Here's my favorite.

A very wealthy businessman is finally convinced by his wife to go on a relaxing vacation. In order to ensure that he doesn't keep calling his office, his wife books them a small house on a tiny, extremely isolated, very beautiful island. The island is little more than a small village surrounding a harbor. The house the couple rents has a balcony overlooking both the harbor and the town's central square, where there's a café, a church, and a small grocery. The first full day he's on the island the businessman wakes, pours himself a cup of coffee, and goes to sit on the balcony. Down in the village square he sees a young man leave his home and walk toward the docks. The fisherman loads his nets in a small skiff and rows out to sea. The businessman imagines how peaceful it must be to fish these waters.

Later that same day the businessman and his wife are sitting on the balcony having lunch. He looks down and sees the same young fisherman rowing back to the dock. His skiff is filled with dozens of baskets overflowing with fish. The businessman watches as the fisherman carries his baskets to the grocery, where he sells his catch and buys some groceries. The fisherman goes back to his house. Later that evening, after having dinner on the balcony, the businessman sees the fisherman along with what must be his family—a wife and two young children—strolling to the café. The family melts into what must be the town's entire population. There's laughing, drinking, and singing.

The next day the businessman sees the fisherman go through the exact same pattern. He leaves around breakfast, returns with an incredible catch by lunch, sells it at the grocery, goes home, and then appears at the café with his family after dinner. The day after that the pattern is the same again. After watching this for four days the businessman feels compelled to speak to the fisherman.

On the fifth day the businessman approaches the fisherman after he has sold his catch but before he's gone home. "Excuse me," the businessman says. "Since my wife and I have been renting that house over there, I couldn't help but see you fish every day. You're an incredible fisherman. I'm a very successful businessman, and I think with just a little bit of effort you could become very wealthy."

"What do you mean?" asks the fisherman.

"Well," says the businessman, "if you went back out in the afternoon and fished for a full day rather than half the day you could double your money."

"What would I do with the extra money?" asks the fisherman.

"First you could use it to buy a bigger boat," says the businessman. "Then you could use the even greater profits to buy a second boat and hire an assistant. Eventually you could make enough money so you didn't have to fish yourself."

"What would I do then?" the fisherman asks.

"Anything you wanted," the businessman says. "You could relax, spend time with your family and with your friends."

The fisherman looks confused, and then says, "But that's exactly what I do now."

There are lots of morals you can gain from the story. For me, the message has always been that you can't have it all if you don't have time to do it all. Sometimes doing less actually yields you more.

Assuming I've got you convinced, do not—I repeat, do not—go into your boss's office and say you're not staying late tonight because you've got to take junior to his little league game. Killing your career is an attitude adjustment, not a suicide attempt. It begins by trying to become more like that proverbial fisherman and keeping focused on the ends, rather than the means.

## Why Do You Work?

In order to focus on the ends, you first need to figure out what they are. You need to ask yourself, "Why do I work?"

It's rare that we actually ask ourselves that question. As we discussed in the previous chapter, we've given control over our work lives to others. By not being in charge of our own work life, by not thinking about why we're working, we're acting reflexively rather than reflectively. It's time to change that.

Over the years of asking my clients to tell me why they work, I've been given many different answers. But after looking over my notes and thinking about all my consultations, I've determined that there are really only eight answers. My clients and, I assume, you work for one of these eight reasons:

1. For power

2. For respect

3. For security

4. To travel

5.  To serve

6.  To meet people

7.  To express yourself

8.  For money

Of course, it's not enough to come up with a simple answer to this question. In order to kill your career and get a job you'll need to dig a little bit deeper. Give yourself a few minutes of reflection. Sit in a quiet spot and let your mind run through all eight of these general reasons. Have a cup of tea or a glass of wine. When you think you've decided which of the reasons fits, say it over and over to yourself to see if it feels right. Then take out your notebook or pad and on top of a blank page write the phrase "I work [fill in the blank]." Now let's see what that really means.

## "I Work for Power"

I get this answer a lot from my male clients. Maybe that's because a high percentage of my clients are corporate executives who want to be top dog. Certainly there's a macho element to this answer. (In all my years of practice I've had only one woman tell me she worked for power.) In fact, this is usually what I call a presenting answer: it's an initial pose or posture often covering the actual response. Lots of men think they're supposed to say they work for power. That's why I usually push them further . . . and why I'll push you further if this were your answer.

Okay. You say you work for power. Well, what do you want to do with that power? Don't think about it too much. Just pull out your pad and write down the first thing that comes to your mind.

Most people, when prodded, will say they want to use their power to get or do something else. And that underlying answer is always one of the other seven reasons. For instance, when I pushed Julius Jackson, a fifty-two-year-old client of mine who worked as an official with a labor union, to tell me for what he'd use the power he was pursuing, he admitted it was to gain respect.

After you've come up with an answer to what you want to do with your power, go over the list of the other seven original answers and see which best fits your response. Now edit the phrase on top of the page in your pad or notebook to reflect your underlying answer.

## "I Work for Respect"

Having the respect of others is somewhat important to almost everyone. There are very few people whose egos are so secure (or large) that they truly don't care what others think of them. But if you wrote that you work for respect, clearly it's essential to you. My next question is: Whose respect do you want? Think about it for a few moments and then write the answer down on your pad.

> Julius Jackson, that client of mine who first said he worked for power but then determined he really worked for respect, told me he wanted "the respect of his peers." I asked him whom he meant by peers. He thought about it for a few moments and then said, "The African American community." Julius grew up in a poor household, and put himself through the City University of New York by working as a doorman at night. He be-

came involved with the doormen's union, and after finally graduating college was hired by the union as an organizer. After more than two decades he had moved up to the executive level of the union.

## "I Work for Security"

Security is a very general term. If you wrote that you work for security, you need to expand your answer by getting more specific. Define what you mean by security. Are you referring to financial security—say, having a large nest egg? Or do you mean physical security—maybe living in a low-crime area? Similarly, whose security are you concerned with? Is it just your own, and maybe your life partner's security, or are you concerned with children, parents, and siblings too? Write your more specific answer under the phrase "I work for security."

Andy Welessa was quick to tell me he worked for security. A thirty-nine-year-old product manager with a consumer electronics manufacturer, Andy was married with three children and a fourth on the way. He and his wife rented an apartment in a middle-class area of Queens—in fact, the same neighborhood in which he grew up. While he was concerned with financial security—putting four kids through college was quite a task—Andy's real motivation was physical security. He told me he wanted his children to grow up in as safe a community as possible.

## "I Work to Travel"

It's only in recent years that I learned how important travel is to many people. I think that's because increasing numbers of young people are coming to see me. By young, I mean people between the ages of twenty and thirty-five, many of whom just recently received their bachelor's or master's degrees, and most of whom are still single. I'm not suggesting that the desire to travel is in any way immature, only that it may be more pressing for individuals who haven't taken on a great many other personal responsibilities.

To successfully kill your career you'll need to be more specific about your desire to travel. Where are you interested in going and why? Perhaps you want to travel to Europe's capitals to tour art museums, or maybe you'd like to tour the Caribbean going from beach to beach. Is it the act of traveling that matters most, or what you do when you're in a different place? In other words, is it quantity or quality you're after? Write down your answers.

Travel certainly was a pressing need for twenty-six-year-old Nicole Cohen, who told me she had specifically chosen trade-magazine journalism over public relations because it offered more of a chance to travel widely. In the five years she'd worked for a gaming-industry magazine she had, in fact, been all over the world. She'd attended industry events in London, Paris, Hong Kong, and Cologne, and she was a regular visitor to Las Vegas and to Native American casinos all around the United States. When I asked her to expand on her travel dreams she talked about how she loved experiencing different cultures firsthand and touring sites of natural beauty.

## "I Work to Serve"

Historically, the drive to serve has been powerful, leading people to forgo material comforts, physical safety, even to renounce physical love. Because service is such an abstract, general concept, I think it's particularly important to dig down and come up with more specifics. For example, whom do you want to serve? There are people who want to serve their nation. Others feel the need to be of service to the underprivileged. Some are called to serve God. How do you want to be of service? Do you feel called to provide direct service, say by actually handing out food to the hungry or defending the nation from terrorism? Or are you more attracted by indirect service, say by helping establish a school, or getting involved in local politics?

Dan Connors told me he had always felt driven to serve. After graduating from divinity school he decided to pursue work in nonprofit management. He began working for a small social service agency in a midwestern city. Realizing he needed an advanced degree to move up the organizational ladder, he went back to school and earned a degree in nonprofit management. Dan eventually became assistant director of that agency. Two years later the director left, and when it became clear Dan wouldn't get the job, he moved to a larger nonprofit agency in New York City. When I asked Dan about the specifics underlying his need to serve, he talked a great deal of his experiences in divinity school, feeding the hungry in the decaying downtown of a New England city.

## "I Work to Meet People"

Many people develop personal relationships with coworkers. When you spend hours working together you develop a certain closeness. If the office is a pleasant place, the warm environment encourages friendliness. If the office is a nightmarish place, the shared misery creates strong bonds—sort of like sharing a foxhole. Working hard easily leads to after-hours socializing, whether it's through the company softball team or just sharing a drink after work at the bar around the corner.

Ever since women became a larger presence in the workplace, romantic relationships among coworkers have been common. At a certain point, work replaced school as the best place to meet a mate. The increased awareness of sexual harassment issues may make things more complex and delicate, but many people still meet their life partners at work. If anything, because of all the hours people are spending on the job, the role the office plays in romance is growing.

If you're working to meet people, you'll need to be more specific in order to kill your career. What kind of people are you trying to meet, and what type of relationship do you want to form with them? Are you looking for a special someone who shares your love of theater or film? Or are you hunting for friends with whom you can share a day shopping or a round of golf?

Andrea Lewis told me she was looking for both love *and* friendship. A thirty-four-year-old, recently divorced woman, she was given a consultation with me as a gift by her sister. Andrea had been a stay-at-home mom when married to her husband, a dermatologist. But since the divorce she had taken a job as a clerk-receptionist at another doctor's office, drawing on her experience working in her ex-husband's office. It was, she said, a way for her to get out and meet people. Andrea explained she was looking for a man who shared her love of the outdoors and culture and friends who enjoyed going to classical concerts and readings by writers.

## "I Work to Express Myself"

For a long time I couldn't figure out why so many of my clients, when asked, told me they worked to express themselves. I don't think New Yorkers are, by and large, any more artistic or creative than anyone else. Slowly I put the pieces together. I see so many people who work to express themselves because they represent an unusually large percentage of those who are the most unhappy at work, and as a result, seek out my help.

One reason those who work to express themselves are so unhappy is that they are often the least-paid workers. Everyone knows the stories of millionaire painters and novelists. But for every one of those millionaire painters there are millions of people earning very little doing some type of graphic art or design work. For every one of those millionaire novelists there are millions of people barely scraping by doing some type of journalism or communications work. Bosses seem to have realized that all they have to do is give people an opportunity for just a little bit of self-expression and they can get away with paying them next to nothing.

But I believe there's another reason creative workers are so unhappy: they face the longest odds in achieving their work goal. Those who work for power, for respect, for security, to travel, to serve, or to meet people have decent odds of at least partly achieving their goal. Those who work to express themselves have, truth be told, little chance of even partly achieving their goal. That's not because they're untalented, necessarily. It's because work simply isn't cut out for self-expression. Work and self-expression go together like hot dogs and peanut butter.

This will be a vast oversimplification, but let me try to explain. Work is a mercantile process. You are paid to produce a good or a service that is of value to others. The more people value whatever it is you produce, the more you are paid. In effect, work rewards mass appeal. Self-expression, on the other hand, focuses on what's valuable to the creator. You produce a good or service that is of value to you. The more it fits your own unique personal needs and wants, the more "value" it has. In effect, self-expression rewards individual appeal. It's not impossible for them to coexist—it's not like a comic book in which two alternate worlds can't come together or else the universe explodes. Instead, it's like putting peanut butter on hot dogs. They just don't go together.

That doesn't mean you shouldn't pursue your self-expression goals. To do that effectively, however, you'll need to be more specific. How do you want to express yourself? Do you like to write? If so, what type of writing? Do you have a particular audience in mind, or is it simply for yourself? You should make the same kind of analysis of any other artistic endeavor.

When I told Sean Shanahan about my peanut butter and hot dog analogy he just shook his head. "I don't eat either, I'm afraid," he said with a chuckle. "But I understand what you're getting at." As I mentioned earlier in this chapter, Sean admitted to having always chosen art over commerce throughout his career. He and I discussed his drive for self-expression in a bit more depth. While he had worked in a number of mediums in his work life, Sean's preferred method of personal expression in the past had been the mixed-media collage. He enjoyed shaping a unique piece of art using a variety of different, often unusual materials. Unlike at work, where he had a clear idea of the target market for all his graphics, his collages were made to please himself.

## "I Work for the Money"

In all the years I've been giving career advice to clients, no one has ever started off by telling me he or she works for the money. A handful, when prompted by my own admission that I work for the money, will say, with some embarrassment, that they too are more focused on what they earn than on what they do.[5] Most, however, seem shocked by such an attitude. At least at first.

Not only is there nothing wrong with working for the money, but it's the approach I believe almost everyone should take. That's what I mean by killing your career and getting a job instead. Rather than viewing your work as a career—something you do for power, for respect, for security, to travel, to serve, to meet people, or to express yourself—you should view your work as a job: something you do for the money. This doesn't mean quitting your current position tomorrow. It's an attitude adjustment that may or may not lead to a change in employment. That remains to be seen after we go through the remaining steps in this book. For now it means changing your orientation toward work from the aesthetic to the mercantile.

Far from asking you to reject your higher calling, I'm doing my best to help you achieve it. You haven't achieved it yet, have you? Despite your stated goal of, say, working for others' respect, you don't feel like you've got it yet, do you? I didn't think so. Otherwise you

5. If you're one of those handful, welcome to the club. Don't be ashamed; you're in good company. You're also in great shape for taking charge of your work life. While you could just jump on to the next chapter, I'd suggest you continue reading this chapter. If nothing else, it will reinforce your already efficient attitude and make you feel even more secure about your mercantile approach to work.

wouldn't be reading this book. You picked this book up for the same reason people come to see me in my office: you're unhappy with your work life. Well, by working for the money you'll become much happier. Let me explain.

There are different ways other than work to achieve every one of the other goals we've discussed. It's easier to satisfy your need for service by spending time feeding the hungry at a soup kitchen, for example, than by trying to find a job that somehow helps the hungry. The mercantile aspect of the job will, by its very nature, impinge on the spiritual element of feeding the hungry. Let's say you're working at a social service agency. You'll need to deal with the politics inherent in any organization. Depending on your position you'll need to negotiate pay raises for yourself from superiors, deal with the petty squabbles among coworkers, train and discipline subordinates, fight to get resources for your department, go out and solicit funds, and perhaps even deal with insurance companies or local governments. If, on the other hand, you volunteer at the soup kitchen run by the agency, all you need to do is feed the hungry. You'll be able to experience firsthand the satisfaction of feeding the hungry, see the joy your work is bringing to poor children, and return home at the end of your time there feeling justifiably good about yourself and your contribution to society.

The same is true for every other reason you may have given for working. There is probably a more efficient way of achieving your goal, one that, in fact, guarantees you'll achieve it. In some cases there might be many other ways of achieving your goal. You can express yourself by acting in community theater, for instance, rather than trying to make it as a professional actor. You can meet people by going to church, or joining organizations, rather than just at the office or plant.

Work, on the other hand, is the single best way to earn money. That is its designated purpose. Ask work to do more and you court dis-

## THE INHERITANCE MYTH

Forget those fantasies about inheriting big bucks from your folks. In the early 1990s an academic study suggested that the baby-boom generation would receive the largest inheritance in history—almost $10 trillion—and that this money would impact a very broad segment of American society. The news spread like wildfire. I had clients come to me for help with inheritance planning . . . even though their parents were alive and well. However, the idea of widespread patrimony is a myth. The numbers were calculated in 1989 dollars, so decades' worth of inflation weren't taken into account. Gifts to charity and to grandchildren weren't taken into account. Increases in the spending pattern of older Americans weren't factored into the mix. Those "We're spending our kids' inheritance" bumper stickers are prophetic. Finally, the study didn't take into account the increased longevity of older Americans and the rising costs of nursing homes, in-home care, and end-of-life health care. I tell almost all my clients they've a better chance of winning the lottery than of inheriting large amounts of money. Stop dreaming about tomorrow's inheritance and instead start leading your life today.

appointment. Sure, there are ways other than work to earn money: you can inherit it, or you can have so much money saved and invested that you can live off unearned income. But relying on inheritance isn't a very good idea. Despite some predictions in the early 1990s, it's unlikely we'll see a huge transfer of wealth between generations. (See the box above: The Inheritance Myth.) And if you're reading this book you're almost certainly not independently wealthy.

My suggestion, then, is to work to earn money and spend the rest of your life pursuing your other goals. To paraphrase the Gospels, render unto work that which is work's—earning money—and render unto life that which is life's—everything else. I also believe in turning around a recently coined adage: Do it for the money and the love will follow.[6]

## "But What About All the Time I Spend at Work?"

Whenever I preach working for the money to a client, I get the same response. It's a variation of the following: "But I spend so much time at work, shouldn't I do something that offers more than financial rewards?" My answer is simple: Stop spending so much time at work.

Most people who come to see me, and I'd wager most of you reading this book, have forgotten the reason for spending so much time on the job. The idea was that because you were doing something meaningful, something emotionally, psychologically, or spiritually rewarding, you'd *want* to spend more time at work. The additional time was supposed to be in response to the nonfinancial rewards you were receiving. But as time has gone on, the reason has morphed.

Spending so much time at work became a sign you weren't a moneygrubbing hourly worker. You were a careerist. You didn't have a "blue-collar attitude," you had a "white-collar attitude." That implied you were educated and a member of the elite, not one of the hoi polloi. Those added hours showed you were pursuing a higher calling than just money. You cared about the company. Then the rationale morphed again.

6. Apologies to Marsha Sinetar, author of *Do It for Love and the Money Will Follow*. Many of the people who cite this adage don't seem to have actually read the book and so misinterpret what Ms. Sinetar is saying. Her point, I believe, is that by doing something you love, your need for money will be lessened. She's really saying: "Do it for the love and you'll be happy with whatever money follows."

## BE LIKE A REAL FREE LANCE

In the Middle Ages, mercenaries were hired by the Italian city-states to wage war on each other. They were known as *condottieri* in Italian. In English they were called free lances. While they were loyal, tough, professional soldiers, they were, according to most military historians, more interested in getting paid than in actually fighting. After all, you don't want to get on the bad side of future potential employers or coworkers. Freelance warfare involved far more maneuvering and clever ruses than actual bloodshed. I think all employees today should take a lesson from these original free lances. Do everything you can to make your boss successful, but don't mess up your own future employment opportunities in the process.

You spent so much time at work because everyone else did. No one left at 5:00 p.m. Fitting in meant working long hours. If you didn't work those long hours, people looked at you somewhat askance. What's wrong with you? they thought. Aren't you ambitious? Aren't you a team player? Don't you love what you're doing?

The fact is almost no one loves what he or she is doing today. But no one, other than those who work for the money, seems willing to admit it outside of my office, or his or her therapist's office. What's so good about being a loyal soldier at work? Loyalty cuts both ways, and most employers haven't shown loyalty to their employees for decades. People today need to be free lances, not loyal soldiers; they do their best for their employer, but their prime loyalty has to be to themselves. (See the box above: Be Like a Real Free Lance.) Those who put the company's interests ahead of their own are just as likely to be terminated . . . and less likely to get reemployed quickly. Those who work for the money are plenty ambitious. It's just that their ambition isn't to move up the ladder, it's to be happy.

I ask you, isn't it crazy to spend most of your time doing something you don't love and for which you get little reward, when you could be spending that time doing something you do love and from which you'd get tremendous satisfaction? My message is to work as long as you must to do your job and collect your paycheck, and then go home and have a life.[7] Not just any life, by the way, but have the life of which you've always dreamed.

## Killing Your Career

In order to kill your career and get the life of your dreams you need to expand on the self-analysis you did a bit earlier in this chapter. Turn back to the page on which you've described and then expanded on the reason you work. Flip the paper over, and across the top of the page write, Ways to Get What I Want. Next, start listing all the various ways you can think of to obtain the goal you've determined is your reason for working. Don't censor yourself. Be as open-minded and freethinking as you can. This isn't a test and there are no right or wrong answers. Right now you're looking for multiple options, not a single solution.

I'd love to help you think outside the box and come up with fresh ideas, but obviously that's impossible in a book. Instead, why not turn to your family and friends for help? Pick people you know will be supportive of your goals, rather than someone who's likely to shoot you down because of jealousy or some preconceived notions of who you should be and what you should do. For instance, if your mother criti-

---

7. Worried your boss won't let you have time to have a life? After putting in practice the techniques I'll offer in subsequent chapters, you'll be able to work from nine to five . . . and still be your boss's most valued employee.

cizes your every move, don't go to her for help in brainstorming. Choose your supportive friend instead.

Set aside a specific time for this conversation, perhaps after taking the person out to dinner or having her over for a home-cooked meal. That will ensure you get her undivided attention and she'll feel a bit compelled to help you, since you've just fed her.

For an idea of how those dialogues could go let's go back through the examples I used earlier and see what those individuals came up with in their conversations with me. I'll take their stories through to the conclusion to show you what kind of successes are possible by killing your career. However, you don't need to get that far along right now. Instead, focus on coming up with what you think is a surefire way to achieve your goal.

## Earning Respect Off the Job

Julius Jackson determined he worked for respect. In particular, he wanted the respect of the African American community. While his position as an executive officer in the doormen's union was inarguably deserving of respect, it obviously wasn't providing Julius with the satisfaction he wanted. He and I worked together for hours on the telephone coming up with other ways he could get the respect he wanted. He jokingly told me he was too old (and short) for the NBA and couldn't carry a tune or dance a lick, so sports and entertainment were out. Julius wasn't much of a churchgoer, so he ruled out becoming active in a congregation. Getting politically active was one possibility, since he'd developed a number of political contacts over the years. The idea that seemed to strike the loudest chord was getting involved in charitable service. After a few months of exploration Julius joined the board of the local youth bureau in the New Jersey city where he lived. Drawing on his contacts with the building trades and local land-lords, he eventually established a summer jobs and apprenticeship program for local youth. Today, Julius is still an officer of the union, but he's happier than ever. His work with the youth bureau has won him kudos from the community. And he recently learned he will be honored as man of the year by a local chapter of Kappa Alpha Psi, an African American service-oriented fraternity.

## Finding Security Away from Work

Andy Welessa knew right away that he worked for security. With three children and a fourth on the way, and a good but not great job as a product manager with a consumer electronics firm, the thirty-nine-year-old Andy knew he wasn't likely to achieve the kind of financial security possible for peers with smaller families. He told me his real drive was the physical security of his wife and children. Andy and I brainstormed about what he could to achieve that security. He could send his children to private schools or move his family into a different part of New York. The family could also make a more dramatic move to an area Andy perceived as safer. That's what the Welessas did eighteen months after Andy first came to see me. Andy arranged a transfer within his company to a job as a manager at an assembly plant in a southern state. His pay stayed the same, but since the cost of living was so much lower, he and his wife were able to afford to buy a home. When last we spoke on the telephone Andy told me how much happier he is seeing his children run around a big country field rather than a paved school yard.

## Traveling for Pleasure, Not Business

Nicole Cohen, the twenty-six-year-old trade-magazine journalist who had been traveling the world for her company, figured out why her wanderlust was still unsatisfied. Her dreams of traveling to foreign countries involved far more than just seeing the insides of airports, casinos, and conference centers. And the foreign cultures she longed to immerse herself in weren't those of hotels and expense-account-oriented restaurants. Yes, she was physically traveling, but it wasn't the type of experience she craved. Together, she and I came up with a number of ways she could achieve her goal. She could take a job with an airline or cruise line. She could work as a guide for an outfitter or a tour company. She could become a freelancer and work on travel articles for publications. We soon realized the problem with those options was that Nicole would still be traveling for business rather than pleasure, and she'd be unlikely to get to do what she really wanted. That's why she settled on another option: going into public relations and traveling extensively on her own. After a yearlong search, Nicole was able to get a public relations job with a large hotel in Florida. The job requires her to work extended hours during the winter, spring, and fall, but offers most of the summer off. That's time Nicole plans to use to travel.

## Serving Others Hands On

Dan Connors's desire to serve was being stifled by the demands of management. While he was doing well working as a top executive at a large New York City–based nonprofit agency, he felt something was missing. He knew he was helping his agency, which focused on the needs of poor New Yorkers, do good. It was just that his days consisted largely of managing personnel, meeting with the media, and lobbying municipal officials. He felt removed from the organization's mission. Dan and I discussed other ways he could be of service without its involving work. He could take a more hands-on approach to developing programs in his agency, or another agency. He could go back to school for social work. That would take time out of his life and cost him a great deal. He could get involved in local politics, helping candidates who reflected his view get elected. But that could be even more frustrating than his work. Or he could work through his church to help the needy. Dan went to the board of his agency and explained that he needed to spend more time doing hands-on service to feel complete. He explained that he would no longer be able to attend meetings or events on Wednesday and Friday evenings, since that was when he would be working at a soup kitchen his church had established.

## Meeting People in the Right Places

Andrea Lewis laughed when she said she wasn't having much luck meeting the kind of people she wanted to meet at her job: "I guess the odds are pretty long for me to meet a classical-music-loving backpacker at a dentist's office." While she *had* met some very nice people and struck up a couple of friendships, the thirty-four-year-old Andrea still felt lonely. She and I tried to come up with some idea for how she could meet people who shared her interests. Even though she doesn't play an instrument, Andrea has joined the local chamber music society and is helping out at concerts by taking tickets and seating guests. She has signed up for a poetry workshop at the local college. And she has joined a local organization that helps maintain hiking trails. She just had her first date in three years, with a man she met while cleaning a trail in a nearby state park.

## Art for Art's Sake

Despite having, throughout his career, chosen work he thought would be artistically challenging rather than financially rewarding, Sean Shanahan still didn't feel he was expressing himself fully through his work at the design firm. He and I talked of ways he could do just that. Sean thought about going back to graduate school for studio art, but he didn't think having someone else tell him what to work on would be particularly fulfilling. He considered staying at an artist's colony over his summer vacation, but realized that would be only temporary. Finally, he thought about turning his home office into a studio. It took only one trip to an art-supply store for Sean to be able to convert a space designed for work he brought home from the office into a space designed for him to do his own artwork. He has sworn off bringing work home over the weekend, reserving his perfectionism for his own work, realizing he could do acceptable professional work during the eight hours a day he spent at the office. At home he is spending time working on his own collages. He has finished six, which he plans to enter in a juried show.

## Turning Work and Life Around

By killing their careers my clients have succeeded in becoming much happier with their lives. Since they're now not placing the burden of providing emotional as well as financial rewards on their work, they're actually feeling better about their jobs. Not only are their expectations lower, but they're no longer as emotionally tied to their offices. They're able to leave work at the office when they come home at night. And by pursuing their nonfinancial goals through the nonwork parts of their lives, they've been much more effective at fulfilling those needs. They've won respect, found security, traveled, met people, and been able to express themselves, to a degree that wouldn't have been possible if they had remained focused on having careers. What has worked for them can work for you. By killing your career and getting a job instead, you'll be able to lead a far richer life.

Of course, it's essential that your current or future employer not realize you're now working to live, not living to work. That's not as difficult as you might think. All you need to do is realize there's no I in job.

# CHAPTER 4

# There's No I in Job

*I'm the boss, you're an idiot. You're the boss, I'm an idiot.*

—RUSSIAN ARMY SAYING

AMY DORRIT HAS become the apple of her boss's eye. She's now able to leave early on Thursdays to pick her son up from day care. During two recent rounds of layoffs, Amy has been assured she's safe, despite her relative lack of seniority. And her last performance review was glowing. It wasn't always this way. During the first year she worked at the law firm as an administrative assistant she felt besieged. Her boss, a young partner specializing in entertainment law, gave her nothing but grief, even though Amy was diligently doing her job, working overtime, and even offering suggestions to improve his efficiency. It was only after she stopped concentrating on doing *her* job and started focusing instead on what would make her boss's work life easier that she began to flourish. Now an expert at shielding her boss from the other partners and at keeping the firm's procedures from interfering with his work style, she's as secure as anyone in the firm, even though she rarely stays late and is, in fact, constantly looking for other work. The same can be true for you.

You can make your position as secure as possible, without spending every waking moment at the office.

You can fire your boss and kill your career . . . and still be a star in your boss's eye, winning effusive praise and support.

You can get raises and promotions and kudos, even though you're actively looking for other jobs.

How can you pull off this apparent dichotomy? Simple: accept the third element in my workplace philosophy: There's no I in job. That's my version of an old coaching cliché, which said that there was no I in team, meaning you should set aside your personal interests and instead focus on the success of the team. When it comes to work, you need to (at least outwardly) set aside your personal interests and focus, not on the success of the company, but specifically on the personal success of your boss.

## There's No Justice in the Workplace

I know this flies in the face of everything we've been told or taught. From an early age we've been led to believe that helping the company or organization you work for do well will lead to success on the job. The more you contribute to the company, the higher up the ladder you'll climb and the more money you'll earn. Everyone from parents to pundits continues to preach this as an ironclad rule. Many advisers actually encourage people to spend their spare time and energy looking for ways to boost their company's bottom line.[8] Once again, I hate to shatter such a pretty illusion, but this truism is nothing of the kind.

Unless you've been in suspended animation for three decades you already know that being good at your job doesn't provide job security, let alone advancement and salary increases. Plenty of people who are very good at what they do have been let go, and continue to be laid off every day. Skill is just about the last thing most employers look at when picking people to fire. Having possible grounds to sue the company and earning less than anyone else are the only two attributes that seem to provide much protection anymore. I said skill was "just about" the last consideration when picking people to terminate, because even lower on the list of factors is contribution to the company.

There is no more justice in the workplace than there is in life. Bad things happen to good people and good things happen to bad people. People who contribute to the company's bottom line are fired every single day. Meanwhile, people who generate little if any profit not only keep their jobs but get promoted. Think I'm being too cynical? Well, before you disagree with my assessment, take a moment to think back to all the jobs you've had over the years. How many times have you found yourself working for someone who you thought was incompetent? Maybe it was a supervisor who never met a deadline, whose management skills were atrocious, and who never came up with an independent idea. And how many other times have you seen someone promoted who obviously didn't deserve it? Perhaps it was someone with less experience, enthusiasm, or expertise than the other candidates.

We've all been in this situation during our working lives. Some of us have seen it numerous times. Many of us are dealing with it right

8. I have to admit that I too was one expert who preached this, until I saw the light.

now. Yet romantic idealism is so ingrained in most of us that we ignore the evidence staring us in the face and instead continue to believe the pundits when they say being a star performer for the company will lead to success. I think it's time to take off the blinders and deal with the workplace as it really is.

Don't worry, it isn't an irrational place impossible to navigate. It's just that you've been using the wrong kind of map. Once you adopt a new map and compass you'll be able not only to find your way, but to prosper as never before.

## It's Your Boss, Not the Company That Counts

For years philosophers and theologians have tried to explain why it is that bad things happen to good people and good things happen to bad people.[9] The explanations have ranged from the sublime—the ways of God are unknowable—to, in my opinion, the ridiculous—there are some who God has predetermined will prosper regardless what they do on earth.

Similarly, the handful of people who've been willing to admit there's no justice in the workplace as well have tried to come up with their own explanations. One famous theory is the Peter Principle, which says individuals in an organization will continue to rise in a hierarchy until they reach a position where they are incompetent. This sounds accurate at first, but doesn't account for those incompetents who continue to advance or those who are competent yet are never able to climb the ladder.

I think there's a better explanation for why there seems to be no

9. Apologies to Rabbi Harold Kushner, author of *When Bad Things Happen to Good People.*

justice in the workplace. Rather than ability or productivity being the vital ingredient for success, it's really meeting your boss's needs or wants. Being good at what you do is important, but only for your self-image and personal satisfaction. The same goes for being productive for the company. To be happy and successful on the job you actually need to make your boss happy and successful. By putting your boss's goals first, you actually put your own goals first.

Truth be told, I don't think many managers put the interests of the company ahead of their own. Most care primarily about themselves. They want to get as much money as they can for as little work as they can. I think this is true of everyone from a department manager up to the chairman of the board. Just look at the recent corporate scandals. Company officers cared more about their compensation packages than the company's profitability. Board members and shareholders cared more about the value of their stock than the company's solvency. The people who succeed in a company are those who realize this and use it to their advantage.

I wouldn't characterize this as being either moral or immoral. Companies aren't living creatures; they are amoral legal constructs. It's the people who work in the company that count, and they behave as people always behave. It's simply human nature to reward and protect those who help you meet your needs. People at work will help you if you have helped them, or will help them in the future. On the other hand, people at work will try to hurt you if you have, or may in the future, hurt them.

Working long hours won't make your job secure. Being the best in the world at your job won't guarantee you won't be laid off. Generating profits for the company won't ensure you'll be rewarded. Conversely, not working overtime won't get you fired. Being only adequate at your job won't make you a candidate for future cuts. And not boosting the bottom line won't keep you from advancing. The only thing that matters is helping your boss meet his or her goals. Do that and you will be the last person your boss lays off and the first person your boss rewards, regardless of the quality of your work or how often you stay late. Ignore the boss's goals and, no matter how good your work and how often you work overtime, you'll be a prime candidate for termination. Put your boss first and as he or she advances in the company, so will you. If you don't meet your boss's needs you'll always be one day away from unemployment.

## Janet Crosetti Faces Workplace Reality

If you recall from chapter 1, Janet Crosetti is a thirty-seven-year-old client of mine who returned to work as a schoolteacher after her daughter went to school. She landed a job as an English teacher in a suburban junior high school. Janet's natural enthusiasm and zeal led her to try to energize a department made up mostly of older teachers very set in their ways. She had six years of pent-up teaching energy and she wanted to use it. During her first few months on the job she was like a tornado, constantly suggesting new lesson plans and, during department conferences, pushing for the use of more multimedia. She was stunned when her first evaluation was mixed, at best. Her department chairman clearly was unhappy.

After Janet told me about her situation, I explained what I thought was happening. I said Janet was focusing on the needs of her students. What she needed to do was to concentrate on the needs of her boss, the department chairman, instead. That didn't mean not helping her students. It just meant doing so in a way that very noticeably met her boss's goals as well. What Janet had to do was figure out what her boss's needs and goals were.

We'll get back to Janet's story later in this chapter, but first let's explore how to figure out a boss's needs and goals, since that's your next step as well.

## What Does Your Boss Most Need and Want?

You can't simply ask your boss what he or she needs and wants. Rather than hearing the truth you'll instead get some platitudes about the company's success or your giving 100 percent, platitudes that probably fly in the face of the facts all around you. Instead, you need to do some intelligence gathering.

Find yourself a small notebook or pad that you can surreptitiously use while at work. On the first page, write a to-do list for yourself, and on the second page compile a shopping list for a trip to the grocery store. These pages serve as camouflage for your real notes, diversions you can show to people if they ask what you're writing. On a subsequent blank page, start keeping track of the things your boss does during the day. Again, forget about what he or she says and instead fixate on actions; it's deeds not words that matter. Make note of your boss's mood swings during the day and what he was doing just before his mood changed. Pay careful attention to what she does to please her own boss and how she reacts to those demands. Don't ignore nonwork issues. If your boss is always looking for people to go to lunch with him, that's an important signal.

Try to compile a week's worth of observations. If you feel it was, for some reason, an unusual week—say your boss's boss was on vacation—take notes for an additional week. After taking notes for one or two weeks, read them over. Now, think back over your past experiences with your boss. If there are any typical scenarios that come to mind that you haven't noticed in the past week or two, add those to your list. When you're sure you have an accurate picture of your boss's actions, you can stow your little notebook for the trip home.

Set aside an afternoon at home to analyze your observations. Take out the pad you used for the exercises in earlier chapters, and head a blank page My Boss's Needs and Wants. Go over each observation, asking what your boss got, or tried to get, out of every action, and write down your analysis on the pad.

Let's say your boss asked someone to pick up his lunch on Monday, someone else to drop off his dry cleaning on Wednesday, and you to give him a lift to get his car at the service station on Friday. What did your boss get from these actions? Help with his personal chores. So you would write down that one of his needs is to have someone be his personal assistant, not just his work assistant.

Perhaps you notice that your boss gets into a funk every Tuesday afternoon just before he has to attend the weekly meeting of department managers. You'd be safe to write down that one of the things he probably wants is to get out of going to those meetings.

By the way, if you simply can't figure out what your boss's needs and wants are, study your boss's boss. Whatever his or her personal wants, every boss needs to please the person above, just as you need to please him or her. So if you can help your boss please his or her boss, you'll be providing a great service. Just make sure your efforts don't come as a surprise. You don't want to appear as if you're going over his or her head.

## Typical Needs and Wants

The list of possible needs and wants is huge, but let me offer some general examples clients and I discovered when analyzing observations. I've developed six general personality types to help you spot your boss's needs and wants. While needs and wants do tend to fall into these groupings, there are no ironclad rules about what bosses are like. You may find your boss fits none of these characterizations, or has needs or wants from two or three different types. This isn't an exact science. Feel free to draw on all of these types, or none, and to mix and match as you'd like. I'm just trying to offer some examples to help you get started in developing your own custom profile of your boss.

*The buddy.* This is the boss who just wants to be one of the guys. He's always asking people to go to lunch with him. Whenever groups of employees gather he wants to be a part of whatever is happening. He wants to join in outside activities and sometimes will even organize. He talks a lot about his personal life, and wants advice on personal matters. He may love to hear himself talk and not be much of a listener, so he needs an audience.

For the past eight years Tim Kalamos has been one of the most productive insurance adjusters in the New York area. A former building contractor, he's expert at assessing how much and what type of repairs will be necessary, and then accurately projecting the costs. Because of his experience, he's also able to write up more reports in a week than almost anyone else at his company. Yet when he came to see me he felt his job was in danger. A new regional manager had taken over and seemed to have it in for Tim. When Tim came to me with his notes on his boss's behavior, we found an interesting pattern. The boss, who had just been transferred to the New York area from the Texas office, was constantly asking people for tips on where to go for lunch, where to shop, what doctors his family should use. Tim and I decided the boss's biggest need was for a buddy who could teach him about life in New York. Tim, a native New Yorker, was perfect for that role.

*The loner.* This is the boss who just wants to do her job and not be bothered with everything else. She's miserable about attending social gatherings or meetings that don't directly pertain to what she does. She issues directives to subordinates and wants not to be asked questions or to have to do any hand-holding. She's wants to avoid small talk and wants new challenges to tackle so she can keep busy.

Jon Halladay is a mechanical engineer working with a consulting firm that specializes in the aviation industry. Having been recruited to work for the firm from a major manufacturer of aircraft engines, Jon thought he'd be greeted as a welcome addition to the firm. But he soon realized the supervisor of the project he was working on was problematic. He came to see me for advice. Jon's discreet notes on the supervisor revealed someone who got angry whenever he was interrupted by a call from the company's management. The supervisor routinely let internal company paperwork slide and seemed to feud with every other manager, from the head bookkeeper to the director of sales. The only time he seemed happy was when he was staring intently at the screen of his workstation. It was soon clear to Jon and me that we were dealing with a loner. To thrive, Jon would need to serve as a gatekeeper.

*The stickler.* This is the boss who carries a huge rule book and needs to refer to it often. He wants everything done according to an established pattern he has set up, either in his head, or on paper if he's an obsessive. He focuses more on how and when things are done, than on the result. He cares a great deal about how the work area and the people in it look to others.

Joan Kent is the daughter of one of the other partners in my law firm. Her father suggested she talk to me about the problems she was having at her first job after graduating college. Joan had studied landscape architecture at a prestigious Ivy League university. Her faculty adviser helped her land a position with a well-known architectural firm headquartered in the northern suburbs of New York. Joan became a member of the staff that drew up plans for the landscaping around the firm's corporate headquarters and shopping-center projects. Being a free spirit and creative, Joan just assumed she'd find a supportive environment. But rather than getting artistic feedback and input from her manager, all she heard was how her wardrobe wasn't professional, her rendering wasn't pristine, her lettering wasn't clear enough, and her designs didn't fit the firm's style. Eventually, she and I realized her manager, despite being in a creative field, was a stickler.

*The glory seeker.* This is the boss who has to be a hero, even if it means creating the crisis herself. She needs to be at the center of everything. She seeks out flattery. She always needs an audience and loves to hear herself talk. She may be very concerned about her appearance. She is jealous whenever anyone else gets credit or recognition.

Nancy Bell was ready to quit when she first came to see me. She and her husband, a member of the New York City Council, had first come to see me when they purchased their co-op apartment. Now she was looking for advice about her job as development director for a small, specialized museum. A gifted schmoozer with a large social network, Nancy was a very good fund-raiser. Yet her boss, the director of the museum, seemed to have problems with her work. She and I went over her observations. He typically took the slightest snafu—most recently, sitting two antagonistic people at the same table at an event—and blew it up into an epic catastrophe. He then personally intervened, and finally, very publicly talked about how he had saved the museum from disaster. Nancy explained that he did this, not just with her, but with everyone from the curator to the building superintendent. She and I agreed he was a classic glory seeker who needed to be seen as a hero, always riding to the rescue.

*The fighter.* This is the boss who's always seeking conflict. He's confrontational and has to get in the last word. He sets himself and his staff in competition with other individuals, departments, or companies. He seems to thrive on putting others down. He seems to enjoy expressing anger.

I first met Tom Duffy when I appeared as a guest on a consumer news and information program he produced for a fledgling cable channel. He was an easygoing and very professional producer, so I was surprised when he called to tell me he had almost punched his boss the day before. I told him to come right in to see me. Tom was working on a new show at the same network, directly under the executive producer who had created the show. The executive producer, referred to by some as "a programming genius," had actually screamed at Tom in front of the entire cast and crew after a recent show. I calmed

Tom down, walked him through my approach to work, and asked him to prepare an analysis of his boss's actions. When we went over them, it sounded like the man was a maniac. He not only ranted, raved, and insulted everyone from the cameraman to the hosts, but he seemed to have a vendetta against other shows on the network. He was the prototypical fighter boss.

*The coward.* This is the boss who's always afraid. She's frightened of anything new and every potential change. She's always seeing the potential risk or downside; for her there's a cloud around every silver lining and the glass is always half empty. Because she's so fearful she's always blaming others for problems.

When I told Janet Crosetti to figure out her department chairman's needs and wants, she really took the task to heart. She jotted down her observations for a week, and then when she realized there was no departmental staff meeting that week, continued making notes for another week. Janet even went to a PTA meeting and a school board meeting, both of which she knew her boss would attend, in order to observe her in different environments. She said she noticed that whenever a new idea was proposed, her boss reacted negatively, but using a different rationale depending on which audience she was facing. At a staff meeting she said the new idea—one of Janet's proposals—would take too much prep time. At the PTA meeting she knocked down one parent's idea by saying it could detract from the time spent with each child. And at the school board she responded to a question about creating a literary magazine for the school by saying it would be too costly. Janet said her boss's two favorite phrases were "We've always . . ."

and "We've never . . ." Janet needed no help from me to see her department chairperson was a cowardly boss.

## So Many Needs, So Little Time

Once you've figured out your boss's needs, you have a simple mission: do whatever you can to help him or her meet one or more of those needs.

If you've found your boss has one pressing need, your task is clear. But if your boss has multiple needs, you'll have to do some prioritizing. You probably won't be able to meet all the needs you've uncovered, at least not right away. That's not a bad thing, however. Multiple needs offer multiple chances to curry favor with your boss. Once you've learned the technique, you can tackle one after another, growing in your boss's admiration each step along the way. But right now, let's concentrate on deciding which need you should address first.

Back in the 1950s a psychologist named Abraham Maslow developed a theory of human behavior based on needs. (See the box on page 90: Maslow's Achievers And Optimism.) He believed that individuals are motivated by unsatisfied needs, and that some needs must be satisfied before others. He arranged categories of needs into a pyramid shape, which he called the hierarchy of needs. The current model of Maslow's pyramid has eight stages, or types of needs.[10]

10. In the 1950s Maslow's initial model had five stages: biological and physiological needs, safety needs, belongingness and love needs, esteem needs, and self-actualization. During the 1970s the pyramid grew by another two stages, adding cognitive needs and aesthetic needs as two new levels between esteem needs and self-actualization. Finally, in the 1990s, the current eight-stage model was adopted.

## MASLOW'S ACHIEVERS AND OPTIMISM

Maslow's hierarchy of needs has become a favorite of those looking for psychological insights that can be applied in pragmatic ways. That's because, unlike most of the other major psychological theories, Maslow's is an optimistic philosophy based on high achievers. Freud based his theories on his study of mentally ill and neurotic individuals. B. F. Skinner studied how pigeons and rats learned. Both were determinists, seeing little difference between the motivations of humans and animals. Maslow, on the other hand, based his theory on his studies of exemplary individuals such as Albert Einstein, Eleanor Roosevelt, and Frederick Douglass. Maslow didn't believe humanity was destined for an endless cycle of violence and other evils. He theorized that as long as we're able to move toward satisfying our needs, we'll also move toward self-fulfillment and helping others fulfill their dreams. That's an excellent lesson for us to apply to our work lives: learn from the successful and believe your goal is within reach.

At the base of the pyramid are the most basic needs: those that are biological and physiological. These would include the basic needs to sustain life, such as air, food, water, and shelter, as well as being warm, sleeping, and sexual urges. I think it's safe to assume your boss's most basic needs are already satisfied. And to be honest, if one isn't, there's nothing you can do that's appropriate to a work relationship.

Once those basic needs are satisfied, people move on to try to satisfy safety needs. These would be the needs of feeling physically safe and secure. I believe this is the first category of needs you may have to address. While they're not actually physical fears, I believe that any of the needs typical of the cowardly boss fit at this level. If your boss needs to be insulated or protected from change, that's the first need you should address. Maslow's theory is that people will only progress on to one category of needs after having all their "lower" needs satisfied. That means if you try to address a higher-level need than your boss's fear of new things, you'll probably be unsuccessful.

After someone's basic needs are met and he's feeling out of danger, he moves on to address needs of belongingness and love. These would be the desire to feel part of a family or group, to give and receive affection, to have relationships with others. If, for instance, your boss shows signs of wanting to be part of the group or develop friendships, that would be a belongingness need. Here's where most of the buddy-boss needs fall.

When belongingness and love needs are addressed, people next move to what Maslow calls esteem needs. These are the needs to achieve, to have status, and to gain others' approval. You can divide esteem needs into two types: first are those that boost self-esteem, like being good at what you do; second are those that represent the need for the esteem of others, say, wanting to have a good reputation. The loner-boss traits fit the need for self-esteem, while the stickler, fighter, and glory-seeker-boss traits fit the need for others' esteem.

Maslow's hierarchy of needs continues on to include cognitive needs (self-awareness and knowledge), aesthetic needs (beauty and order), self-actualization needs (self-fulfillment and growth), and finally transcendence needs (helping others to grow or become self-fulfilled). However, I don't think any of these steps actually fit into the workplace relationship. In the previous chapter I stressed that you shouldn't look to the workplace for emotional, spiritual, and psychological satisfaction. Well, neither should you try to satisfy these needs in your boss. If he needs self-awareness, he should go into therapy. If she needs beauty, she should take up her brush and paint. And if he needs self-fulfillment and to help others grow, he should go to a house of worship.

Applying Maslow's hierarchy of needs to your goal of securing your job means addressing cowardly-boss needs first, buddy-boss needs second, and only then any of the loner, fighter, glory-seeker, or stickler needs. Turn back to the page on which you've written down your boss's needs and wants. Rank them according to how they fit in with Maslow's hierarchy.

Janet Crosetti, for example, realized that her department chairman exhibited both safety and belongingness needs (she was always looking for someone to go out for a drink with her after school board meetings). Applying Maslow, Janet decided she had to address her boss's safety needs before her belongingness needs. But she still had to figure out exactly how she would go about making her department chairman safe.

## Meeting Your Boss's Needs

There's really no mystery to how to meet your boss's needs. Simply provide what he or she is looking for. For example, if you find that your boss needs to feel like part of the crowd, invite him to every group event you're attending. If she wants to avoid certain meetings, offer to attend them in her place. Let's say your boss wants to be a hero. Well, make sure to give him credit for all your own accomplishments. Maybe your boss is obsessed with her staff's appearance. In that case, dress exactly like her. Have a boss who needs to compete? Find him a target. And if your boss is afraid of risks, help her identify and eliminate new hazards. In most cases, figuring out how to meet your boss's needs will be easy. Let's go back to the six types of bosses I outlined earlier and see how to meet their needs and wants.

*The buddy.* Go to lunch with this boss whenever he asks . . . and ask *him* sometimes as well. Make sure to make him part of every group activity. If all the junior staff are planning to go out for drinks after work on Friday, ask him to come along. If he demurs, saying he doesn't want to horn in, assure him he's not . . . even if he is. Make sure he knows about the plan to form a company softball team, and if he wants to become manager, welcome the idea. When he talks about his wife and kids, listen attentively and ask for more details. If he wants personal advice, offer the best you can muster.

> Tim Kalamos had determined that his boss's biggest need was for a friend who could teach him about, and help him adjust to, life in New York. Tim invited his boss to lunch. Over corned beef sandwiches Tim explained that his brother was a doctor and he'd be happy to get some suggestions from him for a good family physician. Tim's wife was a teacher who could help with ideas about private schools. And, coincidentally, Tim was going to Barneys for clothes at the end of the week. Did his boss want to come along?

*The loner.* Do all you can to help your loner boss avoid others' influence. Offer to run weekly staff meetings on her behalf, providing her with a written memo afterward so as not to bother her. Suggest you'd be happy to attend the monthly after-hours industry get-togethers she loathes. Listen to her orders and follow them, asking for any clarifications in writing only. Say you're willing to show the ropes to the new hire and hold his hand while he learns the job. Bring your boss ideas for new projects and challenges.

> After analyzing his boss, Jon Halladay thought he was a loner whom Jon could serve by being a gatekeeper. Jon offered to serve as the department's liaison with the company's other departments, and to handle all the requests for reports from company management. Jon offered to help manage the routine paperwork to free up his boss's day for engineering work.

*The stickler*. Follow the stickler boss's rules to the letter. Show up on time and, as subtly as possible, imitate your boss's appearance. Follow his favored procedures to the letter, whether or not it's necessary or even productive. It's the process that matters to the stickler, not the outcome, so do things by his book. Whenever a new situation comes up, suggest he establish new rules to follow. Help him codify everything and follow his rules religiously.

It took a bit of persuading to get recent graduate Joan Kent to accept that she needed to follow her stickler boss's rules. Joan gave up her funky wardrobe for professional suits that mirrored her boss's garb. She asked her boss for help and advice in getting her lettering up to snuff. Her most effective move was asking for a meeting with her boss to go over all the architecture firm's landscape style rules and attentively taking notes, and immediately following the rules to the letter.

*The glory seeker*. When working for a glory seeker, make sure every one of your triumphs is attributed to your boss. Ask her often to share her wisdom and advice, alone and in group settings. Flatter both her actions and her appearance. Make sure to ask how she is feeling and what she is thinking, in order to offer her a ready platform.

Nancy Bell decided that the secret to managing her glory-seeker boss was to beat her to the punch. Rather than letting her turn every minor situation into a crisis and then resolve it, Nancy began coming to her with "problems" only the boss could solve. Nancy took to bringing her in to finalize donations that had actually already been finalized, and then made sure to give her all the credit.

*The fighter.* The real key to dealing with a fighter boss is not to become his target. Suggest opponents, both inside and outside the organization. Offer scapegoats and targets for his anger. Whatever type of competition he perceives, do your best to help him win, whatever that means. Encourage him to express his anger by subtly goading him into action.

Tom Duffy had a hard time playing up to, rather than punching out, his fighter boss. Still, after some careful reflection he started working to meet his executive producer's needs. First, he told him how a rival show on another network had stolen one of their potential guests, setting it up as an adversary. Then he suggested that some of the advertising staff inside their own network weren't giving their show its due.

*The coward.* When dealing with a cowardly boss, try to show her that what at first appears to be new really isn't new, and therefore is nothing to be feared. Try to eliminate or mitigate anything and everything that causes your boss fear. Offer to accept the blame whenever she's afraid of something going wrong. Identify risks for her in advance of their becoming immediate problems, and either remove them or show how they can be overcome.

Janet Crosetti resolved to come up with ways to overcome her cowardly boss's fears. Instead of presenting proposals as being her own new idea, she began framing them as modifications of things the department chairman herself had done years earlier. When the chairman was about to deny approval of a new software suite for the writing lab, Janet offered to accept the blame if the board questioned the cost. Finally, prior to the creation of a student film festival, Janet warned about inappropriate subject matter and suggested the department narrowly define the types of film that could be entered.

## Two Ways to Pretest Your Plans

If you're unsure whether your plans for meeting your boss's needs will work, there are a couple of things you can do.

First, look around the organization for someone, anyone, who handles your boss well. It could be a peer of your boss or another employee who's clearly the favorite. Spend a few days paying careful attention to how he or she interacts with your boss. How does she respond to your boss's troublesome behaviors? What does he say when your boss lashes out? Consciously or not, this person has figured out how to manage a problematic boss. Learn from him. By the way, this is also a terrific tool if you're at a loss for ways to meet your boss's needs. Just do whatever the boss's favorite does and you'll be fine.

Second, you can cloak your ideas in a memo that suggests a response to a problem or proposes a new initiative, and see how your boss responds to the memo. For example, you can finger potential rivals in a memo for your fighter boss and see if that diverts his anger away from you and marks you as an ally. Or you can write a memo that spins your new idea as actually being a very subtle updating of your boss's brilliant original concept of years back, and see if that assuages the cowardly boss's fears. (See the box on page 97: Janet Crosetti's Memo.) Although the written word is actually more permanent than the spoken word, its impact on your boss's perception of you is much shorter lasting. That means if you were off target you won't have to suffer for very long. If your written trial balloon works, follow it up as soon as possible with a similar face-to-face effort to solidify the positive perception.

---

> ### JANET CROSETTI'S MEMO
>
> Here's an excerpt from Janet's memo to her department chairman:
>
> *To spice up my classes this year I spent some time going back over some of the great things the department has done in the past. I came across information on a terrific diary-writing exercise you used in your classes. If you don't object I'd like to use your idea in my classes, just substituting the design and writing of blogs (Web logs) for the diaries. I'd love to speak with you to get your advice on what parts of the diary exercise worked best, and what you did to make it so successful. I can speak anytime after 2:00 p.m. this week.*

## Isn't This Obvious Brownnosing?

At some point in my discussions with clients they usually have some reservations about working to meet their boss's needs.

Many will hesitate about directly doing whatever it is their boss appears to want. "Won't it be obvious?" they ask. "My boss will see right through it and I'll be in a worse situation than I am now," they worry. I know that's what lots of people think, but, in all honesty, people never see through these efforts. Why? Because there's nothing to see through. You are actually trying to help them meet their needs; you're not pretending. Sure, your motivation is to help yourself, but that's not what your boss will see. While you aren't really putting his needs first, he will think you are. That's because he is always putting his needs first. Rather than being skeptical about your motivation, he will like you . . . no, love you.

And that leads right to the other objection. "Isn't this just brown-nosing?" I'm often asked. My answer is, yes . . . but what's wrong with that? You aren't doing anything to harm anyone else. You are helping your boss meet his needs, and in the effort, you're meeting your own. I call that a win-win situation. Even in situations where you are dealing with a fighter boss and you're offering targets other than yourself, you're not initiating the attacks. Those attacks will come regardless of what you do or don't do. All you're trying to do is deflect them from yourself and perhaps steer them somewhere justified.

Most important, this type of behavior works. A recent survey of executives conducted in the *Wall Street Journal* showed that, in retrospect, all had been swayed by subordinates who played up to them in one way or another. The key words are "in retrospect." All the executives admitted that, at the time, they didn't think it was flattery or, if you like, brownnosing. And when pushed, most of the executives admitted that they behaved similarly in their climb to the top. That's because it works.

By working to meet the needs of your boss you do further your own goals. By appearing to put him or her first you actually put yourself first. Don't have any moral qualms over these kinds of actions. Remember, you're not at work to save the world or to further your art. You're working to make money. I don't think you should feel any guilt over this. But in the off chance you do, you'll have plenty of time to make up for it with all the free time you've gained by putting your boss first.

Don't use up all those extra hours, however. Because from now on you're going to be spending part of every week, even every day, fishing for a new job. You'll cast your net in the next chapter.

# CHAPTER 5

# Go Fish

*If one does not cast a big net, one cannot catch big fish.*

—CHINESE PROVERB

FOR THE FIRST time in his life Joe Gargery has a choice of jobs. Joe's a mild-mannered guy. In fact, his wife sometimes accused him of being not sufficiently aggressive at work. In the past, Joe always waited until his current job became intolerable, or he was let go, before looking for work. And then he was usually so desperate that he took the first job he was offered. But in the last year, despite the economy's being in the doldrums, Joe has been offered two different new positions while still holding his job as a field technician with a cellular telephone company. Joe is in the enviable position of deciding whether to take one of the two offers, or to hold on to his current job. While he's still undecided about which job to take, he's certain that from now on he'll be approaching the job market like a commercial

## ARE YOU ABOUT TO BE FIRED?

There are always signs you're about to be fired. Most people, however, fall into denial and refuse to pay attention to them. By the time you finish reading this book you'll be a practiced job fisherman, so you'll always be looking for work. But until then here's a checklist for spotting impending termination. Check off every box that applies.

❑   You are asked to compile a report on all your ongoing projects.

❑   You are pushed hard to finish one or two specific projects.

❑   You are encouraged *not* to do your usual long-term planning.

❑   You're neither informed of nor invited to meetings.

❑   You receive a critical review for the first time.

❑   Your expense reports are questioned.

❑   Your typical expenditures are criticized.

fisherman, not a big-game hunter. Joe will continue to do what he did this past year: constantly solicit job offers rather than setting out, only when necessary, to land a specific job.

Like Joe, you can go from being a despairing, out-of-work job seeker to being someone who is in demand on the job market.

You can shift from taking the first job that comes your way to having your choice of which jobs, if any, to take.

You can stop being a supplicant at job interviews, signaling your weak position to potential employers, and instead become a finicky job shopper who, by playing hard to get, ends up with far more.

❑   Your direct superior keeps his or her distance from you.

❑   Conversation stops when you enter a room.

❑   You have a vague sense of unease.

If you checked one box or none your job is probably safe for the near future. But don't let that lull you into complacency. This is the best time to start your job-fishing efforts, since you've enough time to rely primarily on long-term efforts.

If you checked two to five boxes your job is in danger. Your boss is laying the groundwork to terminate you at a time of his or her choosing, though it may not be for weeks or months. This is the time to accelerate your job-fishing efforts, both short- and long-term.

If you checked more than five boxes you're already fired . . . you just don't know it yet. The decision has been finalized, and you're just a "dead man walking." Unless you've got enough money in the bank to keep you and your family afloat for six months, find yourself a stream of income as soon as possible. It will be easier to get another job while you've still got this one.

Just as with the previous steps in my new approach to employment, the secret to turning your work life around this way is to adopt a new attitude: job fishing.

## The Desperate Hunter

The traditional way people look for work has led to a job search that's reactive, inefficient, and enfeebling.

If you're like most of my clients, you start looking for work only

## CAN YOU NEGOTIATE SEVERANCE?

In a word, yes. There's no legal requirement for an employer to pay a terminated employee severance. However, it's an accepted standard to provide a minimum of two weeks' pay to anyone who has been fired without cause. The problem is the two-week tradition started half a century ago, when it might have been possible to land another job in two weeks. Fat chance doing that today.

That's one reason why you shouldn't hesitate to try to negotiate a larger severance package than the one you're offered. Another reason is that the worst that can happen is they say no. They've already fired you, so what's the risk? Believe me, they won't take back their severance offer just because you ask for more. It's another story if you launch a lawsuit.

Do not sign or agree to anything when you're informed of the termination. The human resources person and your ex-boss will push you to take the check they've already cut and sign a release right then. Resist. Say you're too distraught to comprehend anything and ask for a meeting the next day instead. There's nothing they can do

after you've been laid off or fired. Maybe, if you're like a handful of my more assertive clients, you start looking for work when you pick up signs at work that your job may be in danger, and you refuse to fall into denial. (See the box on page 100: Are You About to Be Fired?) In either case you're in trouble.

Back in chapter 1 I introduced you to Jared Edwards, a client of mine who has been a successful salesman for his entire working life. Beginning by selling photocopiers, then moving on to woodworking and finally music-room fixtures for schools, Jared had always managed to land sales jobs. When he lost one job, for whatever reason, he soon was able to land another. But when the music-fixture firm was pur-

except say yes. Do not say thank you when you leave or shake any-one's hand. Just nod and say, "I'll see you tomorrow."

If you believe you're being discriminated against, call an attor-ney as soon as you get home and let her handle it from there. If you think your termination, while unjustified, is legal, take matters into your own hands.

That night, call your former boss at home on the telephone. Don't ask for your job back. Just say you'd like his support the next day. Lay the guilt on as thick as you can. After hanging up the tele-phone, come up with a counterproposal. Ask for at least a month's severance for every year you've worked for the company, for use of the office for your job hunt, for outplacement counseling, and for the company to pick up the cost of your health insurance until you're reemployed.

Be as businesslike as you can at the meeting. Be ready to do some horse trading. You don't want this to drag on any more than they do. Get as much as you can and get out of there.

chased and its entire sales force was let go, Jared's luck ran out. While he spent hours a day on the telephone, contacting all his old sales net-works, and day after day trolling the Internet for leads, it took him eighteen months to land a job. It turned out that the merger of his former employer was caused by an industry-wide downturn. By the time Jared and the other laid-off workers hit the job market, all the most likely employers were also downsizing, not hiring.

By waiting to be fired, or until you pick up the hints you're about to be fired, you've handed control of the timing of your job search to someone who thinks so little of you as a worker that he has, or is about to, let you go. Believe me, your boss won't be choosing the time of

## ARE YOU ELIGIBLE FOR
## UNEMPLOYMENT COMPENSATION?

Unemployment compensation is a federal program administered by the individual states. As a result, eligibility and the amount received is affected by both federal and state rules. Let me go over the general rules. For specifics you'll need to contact your state's department of labor.

To be eligible you must first meet your state's minimum requirements for wages earned and time worked during the prior year.

You must have been fired through no fault of your own. That means you're not eligible if you quit, were fired for cause, or are on strike.

- ❑ You must be able to work during each day for which you're claiming benefits.
- ❑ You must be available for work immediately.
- ❑ You must have transportation.
- ❑ You must not be required to stay home to care for dependents.
- ❑ You must actively be looking for work.

your termination based on when *you'll* have the best chance to get another job. He will terminate you when it fits *his* needs. He may go to church every Sunday, but he'll fire you on Christmas Eve if he needs you there for the last-minute rush of shoppers, but not after. Whenever he fires you, or starts preparing for it, you can be sure business in your industry or profession will be down, just as it was when Jared was laid off. (See the box on page 102: Can You Negotiate Severance?)

Most bosses hate to terminate people for performance reasons. It's a sign they made a mistake in hiring the person in the first place.

If you quit or were terminated for cause you should try to negotiate with your former employer asking him to say you were fired without cause so you'll be eligible for benefits. The worst he can do is say no.

To maintain eligibility you'll need to report to an unemployment office as often as the state requests to file a claim and show evidence that you've been looking for work. Some states will let you file claims by mail. If you're offered a suitable job you must take it. Otherwise you'll lose your benefits.

What's suitable? Generally the rules rely on common sense. A former comptroller of a company won't be expected to take a job as a fry cook, but might be expected to take a job as a staff accountant.

Benefits generally are 50 percent of what you were earning, up to a ceiling set by each state. Benefits usually last for twenty-six weeks but are sometimes extended because of high unemployment rates.

There are times when layoffs are a legitimate response to economic trouble. But lots of times bosses use a downturn in business as a rationalization for termination so they feel better—"I hate to let you go, Steve, but business is bad." Whether your being canned was a legitimate response to economic doldrums or a rationalization doesn't matter; either way, you'll be left with little chance of finding anything else soon, since all your prime candidates will also be experiencing slow business. (See the box on page 104: Are You Eligible for Unemployment Compensation?)

The average terminated employee then launches a desperate short-term campaign to land a job. My clients would send out hundreds of résumés, make dozens of telephone calls, and send out countless e-mails. Their goal was to land a job as soon as possible. Rather than carefully picking their targets, they flooded the market, contacting anyone and everyone with whom there was a remote possibility of getting a lead or a job. As soon as they got a response, they fixated on that position. They often stopped sending out résumés, making calls, or sending out e-mails, and instead boned up on the company and person with whom they were interviewing. Desperate at not having any money coming in, they usually grabbed the first job they were offered without negotiating.

That's what Jared did. After eight months of not even a glimmer of a new job, Jared had run through all his savings, and then took part-time work as a cabinetmaker to help make ends meet. His wife's civil service job provided health benefits for the family, but things got tight quickly. With his daughter about to start college, his son needing braces, and his wife growing increasingly nervous, Jared felt desperate. When he got a lead on a job selling a computerized reading-education system to school districts, he borrowed money to fly to the company's headquarters for an interview. His willingness to take on a very underperforming sales region cinched the deal, and he grabbed the job when it was offered. As he himself told me, all he cared about was that "the first paycheck didn't bounce when I rushed to cash it."

The metaphor that has been used for the job-search process is a hunt, and it's an apt one. The typical job seeker is like a desperate hunter who decides to set out for game when his family is starving. He heads off into the forest looking for something to shoot and bring back for the family table. It doesn't matter what he finds, as long as it's edible. Reacting in this fashion isn't a very good way to go through your working life today.

## GET USED TO JOB HOPPING

I think it's vital for you to come up with away to deal with the decline in job duration. This isn't just a short-term phenomenon related to the bursting of the Internet bubble or the post–September 11 recession. Those factors had some short-term impact, but the real causes are much more long lasting. The life cycles of products and services are getting shorter, and competition is coming from all over the globe. That has led to a shift in the way businesses are structured. Most jobs today are with small service firms, not large manufacturing companies. Those small firms are more nimble, but far less stable. They probably have no more than three layers of hierarchy and concentrate on just one core function. Since they have little financial cushion, these small firms are much more likely to let people go to compensate for changes in their business. Things are going to get worse before they get better, so if you plan on working in the next two or three decades you'd better adjust your thinking and actions.

## Job Hunting No Longer Makes Sense

Approaching the search for work as a hunt makes sense if you're going to go through the process only a handful of times in your life: when you leave school and get a first full-time job, and then maybe the one or two times you're either fired or have to move to a new location. The job hunt used to be a rare thing, like buying a home. That was the typical pattern for workers decades ago, back when there was corporate loyalty and when you could count on keeping your job if you kept your nose clean and did your work. But that pattern doesn't fit today's world. We know there's no corporate loyalty anymore and that doing your job, even excelling at your job, isn't enough to ensure that you'll even have a job. Looking for a job is no longer something you'll have to do just a couple of times in your life. Today you'll have to do it frequently.

According to the *Economist,* the average thirty-two-year-old American has already worked for nine different firms. The Bureau of Labor Statistics shows that job tenure—the length of time someone stays at a particular job—is dropping, particularly for men aged thirty-five and over, the very individuals who we used to assume were at the most stable period in their work lives. (See the box on page 107: Get Used to Job Hopping.)

The rule of thumb used to be that traditional job hunts took one month for every $10,000 you earned. I've found that today it's taking twice that long. It's taking a person who was earning, say, $90,000 a year about eighteen months to find a new job, using the traditional techniques. And that new job invariably pays less than she was earning before—sometimes a lot less. The market is no better for those earning less, or more.

I have some new techniques that can help cut that time down, which I'll go over later in this book. But the best first response to the new job environment is to abandon job hunting altogether and take a different approach, one I call job fishing.

## The Savvy Fisherman

Rather than waiting to look for a new job until you've been fired, or you've spotted the signs you're about to be fired, you need to be looking constantly for a new job. And when I write constantly I do mean constantly. The job search isn't something you start when desperate and finish when reemployed. It's something that should be a part of your daily work life. Businesses don't stop advertising when they land a customer, and start again when they have no customers—at least smart businesses don't. They advertise constantly, looking to create a steady flow of customers so there's never a time when they're without business. Your goal should be the same: a steady flow of employment offers so you're never without a job.

I used the word "offers" intentionally. That's another part of the job-fishing program. Rather than looking for "a job" per se, you should instead focus on getting job offers. Then, after having been offered a position, you can decide whether or not you want to accept it.

The metaphor I like to use is job fishing, not job hunting. Rather than waiting until there's no food on the table and then setting out to kill anything you can to feed your family, you go out every day, cast very big nets into the ocean, see what you catch, and then sort through the haul, choosing which to keep and which to throw back.

Think about what a difference this kind of approach makes.

If you're always looking for a new job while you're already employed, you'll be under little if any pressure to take a position that doesn't meet your needs and wants. You'll be able to shift jobs at a time when the economy is in your favor: say, when there's a high demand for people with your skills. Rather than the potential employers having the leverage in the situation, you'll be the one with the power. The burden will be on the potential employer to convince you her company is worthy. You will no longer have to go on job interviews with your hat in hand, begging for a position.

Everyone knows that it's easier to find a job while you're still employed. Partly it's because the potential employer sees hiring you as a double positive. Not only does she get your services, but she also gets to deprive a competitor of your services. I think a less appreciated advantage of searching for a job while you're employed is the impact it has on your attitude, and as a result, your presentation. It's human nature to want what you can't have. When you go into a job interview not yet convinced you even want the job under discussion, you broadcast that to the interviewer. Rather than this creating anger, it actually entices the interviewer. That's because you project confidence, not arrogance; and that's intoxicating to a potential employer. (See the box on page 111: How You Should Act on Interviews.) She suddenly is working hard to talk you into taking a job you haven't even been offered. It's remarkable how many times clients of mine come back from interviews for jobs they really didn't want and report that they were offered the moon to take the spot.

Contrast that with the number of times people go into interviews desperate for the job and don't get the offer. I think that's because the interviewer reads desperation rather than confidence. Desperation is not an attractive trait. The best response it can generate is pity, and that's not sufficient for most employers to offer you a position. Instead, he'll feel uncomfortable with your desperation and will cut the interview short just to get out of the situation. An hour later he'll turn around and offer the job to someone who doesn't really want it.

Alex Linderman knows the effect attitude can have on an interviewer. A banquet manager for a large catering operation in the New York suburbs, he has been a client of mine for many years, stretching back to when I first began practicing law. Alex was making an excellent living at the suburban catering hall when, out of the blue, he received a call from the human resources director of a famous old New York City hotel that was being renovated. The hotel was looking for a banquet manager. Figuring he had nothing to lose, Alex went on the interview, even though he didn't want the job, since it would mean a long commute. He blew the interviewer away, and was offered the job on the spot. He called the next day to turn it down, after using it as leverage to get a raise from his current boss. Two

## HOW YOU SHOULD ACT ON INTERVIEWS

The reason why people always come across best in interviews for jobs they don't want is that they're signaling self-confidence rather than desperation. The best ways to do that are behavioral.

Make sure your dress and grooming are impeccable and your cologne and jewelry are understated.

Arrive on time. Being there too early conveys desperation. Being late means you're either rude or disorganized.

Smile, shake hands firmly, and make eye contact with everyone you meet.

Don't sit until invited to.

Lean forward in your chair and maintain eye contact when making a point.

When asked a question, sit back and break eye contact to indicate you're thinking. Then reestablish eye contact and lean forward again when answering.

Don't slouch, cross your arms or legs, or touch your face. Keep your hands from fluttering about.

Don't be afraid to use humor. It's a sign of intelligence and cuts the tension.

Have questions of your own. Make this a give-and-take rather than an inquisition and you'll get an offer.

years later the catering hall on Long Island had been sold, Alex was out of work and desperate, and he got another call from the same hotel in New York. In fact, he was interviewed by the same person. But this time the interview clearly didn't go well at all. In fact, the interviewer asked if Alex had had health problems recently, since he didn't seem like the same person he had met with before.

## "But What If My Current Boss Finds Out?"

When I explain to clients that they need to look for a job while still employed, many express fear that their current boss will find out. I'm sure some of you have that same fear. My response is: "So what? What can your boss do?"

Assuming you've been doing everything you can to meet his needs, as outlined in the previous chapter, his response will be fear, not anger. He'll be afraid he'll lose you and will do everything he can to keep you. Your job fishing will serve as a wake-up call and could lead to your getting a raise, a promotion, or some other perks. He'll do whatever he can to make sure you stay there, keeping him from having to go to meetings he dreads, or bringing him his breakfast every morning and picking up his dry cleaning at lunch.

In cases where it's a toss-up between your current job and a job offer, you should actually come out and tell your boss about the offer. Explain that you were approached about another job, but would prefer to stay where you are now . . . if your boss can meet some of the advantages the potential new job offers. He'll either meet the new offer, or not. If he does, you can stay where you are. If he doesn't, you take the new job.

> Larry Endowsky is an optician who has excelled working in the same optometry office for the past three years. Early on Larry realized that the optometrist owner loved giving exams but hated interacting with patients. As a result, Larry became what he called "the social director" of the practice. He met patients in the waiting room, took them to the preliminary tests, escorted them to the optometrist's office for the examination, and then brought them over to the eyeglass area for

## WHAT TO SAY IF YOUR BOSS FINDS OUT

If your boss finds out you're looking for another job and asks you about it, the best response is confirmation, not denial. You want to act nonchalant, stressing that it was nothing out of the ordinary and that's why you didn't think it merited bringing it to your boss's attention. Then add some superficially reassuring words that also carry a subtext. Say something like this:

*"Yes, I've been contacted about other opportunities. I get calls from headhunters every four or five months. You know I'm not happy with the money I'm earning here, but don't worry—I don't want to leave."*

selection and fitting. Larry was paid comparatively well, but that didn't stop him from looking for work. He was called for an interview for a manager's position with a one-hour eyeglass chain store that had recently opened in a nearby mall. The optometrist's wife saw Larry being interviewed while she was at the mall shopping and rushed home to tell her husband. The next day Larry was offered a raise as well as a share of the business.

Even if you haven't been able to meet your boss's needs before he learns of your job fishing, it will have no impact on your situation. We are all contingent workers today anyway, and no one knows that better than your boss. Don't deny you're job fishing if asked. You've nothing to be ashamed of. You're just being a savvy employee, doing everything you can to solidify your stream of income and explore your options. (See the box above: What to Say If Your Boss Finds Out.)

If your boss continues to express shock at your lack of loyalty, it could be a sign he was thinking of terminating you sometime soon and is upset you're potentially throwing off his desired timing. In that case you're a step ahead of the process by having launched your job-fishing mission ahead of time. You didn't lose anything by looking for a job while still working. In fact, you helped yourself by getting a jump on the process.

## "But What If I'm Offered Two Jobs?"

Another fear expressed by clients whom I tell to "go fishing," which I assume some of you share, is being offered two jobs at the same time. My response is, "Why is that a problem?"

It's really amazing. As employees we have been beaten down for so long that we're afraid of being in demand, rather than being a supplicant. It's like the stories you read of freed slaves after the American Civil War who, having been so psychologically (not to mention physically) beaten down, were frightened of freedom. If you're offered two jobs at the same time that's a good thing.

Can you imagine a business owner saying, "I'm worried two people will want to buy my product"? Of course not: competition boosts revenues. If you need evidence of that, just go online and look at what some things sell for on eBay, the Internet auction site. You can find items that are currently for sale in retail stores being sold at auction on eBay for far more than they cost in a store. Why? Because more than one buyer is interested and the multiple buyers get caught up competing with each other. The same can happen when you go job fishing.

If you receive more than one offer at the same time, and you've still got your current job to boot, you're not facing a problem; you're in a terrific situation. Decide which of the two new offers you find

## HOW TO NEGOTIATE AN INITIAL SALARY

The best opportunity you'll ever have to increase your income is when you're negotiating your initial salary on a job. You are at your most powerful, since you're the potential hero who has to be convinced to come on board.

The secret is to keep your mouth shut. If you put the first number on the table the negotiation will be about lowering your number. If, on the other hand, your potential boss puts the first number on the table, the negotiation will be about increasing her number.

If you're asked how much you're looking for, say you're looking for market value for someone of your skills and abilities. If you're pushed further, don't dance around the issue too much. Instead, offer up a high figure. What's high? Well, hopefully you've done some research. But in any case, you can assume the company has a range rather than a specific number in mind. Any advertised number will represent the low end of that range.

Let's say they are advertising the position for $45,000 or "mid-forties." They were probably paying the previous job holder $50,000. But they're probably willing to pay upwards of $55,000. If pushed to come up with a number, my suggestion would be to say $60,000, in an effort to end up at the high end of the range. Simply rationalize any concessions you must make by saying things like, "Well, I am intrigued by the challenges this job would offer," or "This job would give me the chance to enter a field in which I'm fascinated."

most attractive. My advice would be, as you might guess, to choose the one that offers the most compensation. (See the box above: How to Negotiate an Initial Salary.) Select a few areas where the lesser offer has some advantages, and go back to the person making the preferred offer, subtly asking her to match those advantages. (See the box on page 116: How to Leverage Job Offers.) If it's a toss-up between the

## HOW TO LEVERAGE JOB OFFERS

If you'd like to use one job offer as leverage against another offer, or against your current boss, you should say something like this:

*"As you know, my stream of income is very important to me. From time to time I'm approached by headhunters about positions that are open. I've been offered another position. I would prefer to continue working with you [or, accept your offer], but I need you to know that this other firm has offered me . . ."*

If you're afraid such obvious blackmail could put a bull's-eye on your back, you can have the news come from a third party. Either casually let the office snitch know about your being offered another job, or use a trusted person—a client or the president's secretary—to pass along the news.

winner of the two offers and your current job, go back to your current employer and ask her to meet the new offer.

Do you have a sense now of how much of a difference job fishing can make in your work life? Not only will it let you choose the timing of your departure from a job, and potentially pick and choose from among multiple job offers, but it offers the best chance to dramatically increase your income. The largest salary increases don't come from negotiating regular raises with your boss. Those are generally limited to single-digit percentages not much higher, if at all, than the rate of inflation. Jumps in salary come when you shift jobs or, excuse the term, blackmail your current employer.

Frankie Martin has the rare ability to look at someone and instantly figure out what clothes she should wear to look her best. A graduate of New York City's Fashion Institute of Technology, she's the granddaughter of a neighbor of mine. Frankie took a job as a salesperson in the juniors' department of a large department store, more interested at first in the employee discount than the salary. As each month went by, increasing numbers of young girls from New York's wealthy families were showing up at the store, and specifically asking for Frankie to wait on them. While Frankie wasn't enamored with retailing, she knew the job market was depressed in New York, and so, after a consultation with me, she concentrated her job-fishing efforts in the retail fashion business. She soon received an offer to be an assistant manager at a competing department store. Two days later she received a similar offer from a well-known women's specialty store, run by a former fashion model. When she got back in touch with the department store and expressed reticence, the store changed its proposal, offering to make her a personal shopper for its best young-adult customers. Frankie grabbed the job, which had a salary that was double what she was making.

## "How Do I Balance Constant Job Fishing with Actually Doing My Job?"

The final objection I get when I suggest my clients start job fishing is that it's impossible to look constantly for work while still working. I'll give you the same answer I give them: difficult, perhaps; impossible, no.

First, remember that by looking for emotional, psychological, and spiritual satisfaction from your life, not your work, you won't be spending as much time on the job as before. By making meeting your boss's needs your primary focus, you also won't be under any added

## AVOIDING EMPLOYMENT AGENCY SCAMS

Unfortunately, the employment agency industry attracts more than its share of shady operators, particularly when unemployment is high. Here are some tips for steering clear of the rotten apples.

Make sure to visit their office. Scam boiler-room operations will want to interact only over the telephone or via e-mail.

Check their professional standing. See if they're members of the National Association of Personnel Services, the American Management Association, or the Society for Human Resource Managers.

Beware advance fees. Walk away if it costs money to walk in the door or to take tests. Once an agency has your money it has little motivation to help you further. Pay a fee only if you land a job.

Steer clear of agencies that place fake classified ads or that have 900 numbers.

Don't sign a contract without first reading it thoroughly . . . at home. Watch out for agencies that push you to sign right away, claiming it's "a standard form."

pressure to stay late. That means we're not talking about adding two hours a week to a schedule already filled with sixty hours of work. Adding those two hours of job-fishing time to a typical forty-hour workweek doesn't seem like much of a burden. Especially not when you consider the potential payoff.

Second, a lot of your job-fishing work, as you'll see in the next chapter, can come during your personal rather than work life. I don't mean you need to give up playing golf to go job fishing. Playing golf can *become* job fishing. In addition, you'll also be leveraging your time by having others, particularly headhunters and employment agencies, do some of your job fishing for you.

Third, and last, job fishing needn't be that time-consuming or draining. Since you're not under the time pressures of having to get a job as soon as possible, you can take a more deliberate, planned approach.

That's what I explained to Jared Edwards after he told me about his history of recent employment woes. Jared and his wife had come to see me for help in cleaning up their credit prior to purchasing a home. During the eighteen months Jared had been unemployed the family had relied heavily on credit cards and had then strung some of the banks out by skipping and delaying payments. Their survival efforts had done a number on their credit rating. Jared's natural sales skills had helped him close a few big deals selling the computerized educational systems, despite the shortcomings of his territory, so the Edwardses had been able to pay most of their debts and put some money aside. I spent a great deal of time working on employment with both Jared and his wife. Having so recently suffered through a spell of unemployment, Jared was quick to embrace the concept of job fishing.

## A Job-Fishing Plan

Just as it made sense to plan out your overall work plan, so I think it makes sense to plan your job fishing. Take out your now well-worn pad and head a page Job Fishing. On it, start making notes of all the things you can do to stay abreast of job opportunities.

Turn back to your work plan and note the alternate paths you discovered. Write those, along with your current work path, in a list on your job-fishing page.

Take one morning or afternoon of an upcoming weekend and go to your nearest college library. Sit down with a reference librarian and ask him for help finding the top two trade or professional magazines dealing with each of the work paths on your list. Write those titles down on your pad. Scan some back issues, looking for the names of

## ELIMINATING RÉSUMÉ RED FLAGS

Résumés are human-resources screening devices rather than applicant promotional devices. Their main function is to provide a human-resources person or manager with information he or she can use to cut down the number of potential candidates so interviewing doesn't take too long. That's why I encourage my clients to have a résumé that eliminates all potential red flags.

Ironically, job candidates usually err by providing too much information, not too little.

Begin by removing all dates that could inform the reader of your age. You don't need to list when you graduated college. You also don't need to list every job you've ever held. Pick the handful of jobs most relevant to the one for which you're being interviewed.

If you must offer some kind of objective or brief biographical sketch, make sure it matches what you assume to be the ideal candidate. For example, saying you're looking to "learn" or "grow" implies you're young. Phrases such as "new challenges" or "expand your skills" implies you're older.

Trim your list of skills and achievements to include only those relevant to the job in question. It's counterintuitive, but listing too many skills and achievements may make you seem overqualified or older than the target candidate.

One place you can provide more rather than less information is in a section on personal interests. Employers aren't allowed to come right out and ask about your age, marital status, or physical condition. Some, out of fear, will even trash résumés that provide that information.

You can let them infer a desired age by noting that you're, say, either president of the local chapter of the Phish fan club or the bridge club. Including that you're a marathoner would allay health issues. And reporting that you're treasurer of the church's couples' club and have twice supervised the local PTA fund-raiser says you're married with children.

any headhunters or employment agencies that seem to be active in the fields. Again, make a note of them on your pad. (See the box on page 118: Avoiding Employment Agency Scams.) Spend a few hours searching the Internet for any sites that seem to offer a decent collection of ads relevant to your needs. Write down the URLs.

While still at the library, pick up the most recent issue of your local newspaper that has the most help wanted ads. In most cities, that's the Sunday paper. In towns where there is no Sunday paper it's usually the Saturday edition. If there are multiple newspapers in your community, consult them all. Include weeklies as well as dailies. Go through the help wanted section, looking to see where jobs pertaining to all your job paths are listed. Note the appropriate headings. Once again, look for any headhunters or employment agencies that stand out.

Before you leave the library, compile two lists: one, a reading list of all the trade magazines, Web sites, and newspapers you'll be checking on a regular basis; the second, a contact list of headhunters and employment agencies.

Make it your business to telephone all the headhunters and employment agencies you've listed and inform them of your interest in other work. Set up personal meetings if you can, and certainly follow up with a package including a cover letter and your latest résumé. (See the box on page 120: Eliminating Résumé Red Flags.)

Next, set aside two hours a week to go over the magazines, Web sites, and newspapers on your reading list. You can subscribe rather than go to the library if it's more convenient. You can probably get away with reading the trade magazines while at work, either on your lunch break or when you have downtime. I would not recommend reading the want ads or scanning the job sites at your desk, however. No amount of attention to meeting your boss's needs will make that acceptable behavior: it's far too confrontational and sends a signal that everyone, not just your boss, can pick up.

Obviously you're looking for every relevant want ad in the magazines and newspapers. Answer all of them, since you're casting a wide net for offers, not just jobs. But keep an eye out for interesting articles as well. Perhaps you'll come across a story about a company looking to change its direction, or a firm looking to add new products or services. Maybe there will be a profile of a CEO who sounds interesting. Make note of any such story that piques your interest. Send an e-mail, or if you can't find an e-mail address, a letter, to the individual mentioned in the story, noting where you read about him or her, and explaining how you think it might be mutually productive for the two of you to meet and speak. Do *not* attach or include a résumé. These notes won't always yield a meeting. But when they do, it will be a productive one. And since you're not in any rush—remember, you're job fishing not job hunting—quality rather than quantity is your aim. You're actually looking to create relationships rather than looking for jobs.

After working with Jared for a year we met to take stock. He and his wife were happy in their new home. While sales of the computerized educational system were good, there had been some recent shake-ups in the upper management of his company. Jared had been and still was fishing for offers. In fact, two had come along in the past three months, but neither paid as much as his current job. Still, they had given him some confidence. Meanwhile he had struck up an e-mail relationship with an inventor who lived in his territory. He had seen an article about the man in one of the trade magazines on his reading list and had sent him a note. A somewhat eccentric engineer who had been responsible for a major medical breakthrough some years earlier, the man had just started working on a new form of a superefficient home heating system. Jared told me that while it didn't seem likely to yield a job offer right away, he was traveling to have lunch with the fellow the next week. I congratulated Jared, telling him he'd reached the next stage in developing a new workplace attitude.

That's the same stage you're about to reach. Jared had learned that cultivating personal relationships is more important today than cultivating business contacts. In the next chapter you'll see that today, no one hires a stranger.

# CHAPTER 6

# No One Hires a Stranger

*Never like seein' strangers. Guess it's 'cause no stranger ever
good newsed me.*

—JOHN WAYNE IN *RED RIVER*

AGNES WICKFIELD CAN hardly believe that getting active in
her local chamber music group has led to a new job. For years, Agnes
had been trying to move from her job as a paralegal with a midsize law
firm into the corporate world, which she knew offered better pay and
benefits. Agnes had networked religiously for two years, and had gone
on so many informational interviews that she felt like a journalist. Yet
nothing ever came of them. In fact, it was getting harder to line up
those interviews. Then, early this year, Agnes took a different tack.
She got more active in her church. She began volunteering at the local
hospital. She even dusted off her cello and joined the chamber music
group in town. At a joint Christmas concert with the local choral society, Agnes struck up a conversation with one of the volunteer ushers.
He turned out to be vice president of an energy company headquar-

tered in a nearby suburb. Three weeks later he arranged an interview for Agnes with his company. Two weeks after that she was offered a job as an in-house paralegal.

Agnes learned an important lesson, one I preach to all my clients as the fifth part of my workplace philosophy, and one which I'll be urging you to realize: in today's work world, no one hires a stranger.

No matter how diligently you scour ads, no matter how extensive your network, and no matter how many informational interviews you go on, those traditional techniques alone won't get you a job . . . not unless you're able first to develop a relationship with the person who does the hiring.

Volunteering each week at a local soup kitchen will today lead to better job offers than going to a trade show.

Being an active member of the PTA is today a more effective job-search technique than being an active member of your professional association.

And singing in the annual community Christmas concert will generate more positive job leads than all the informational interviews in the world.

Incredible as it may sound, pursuing your personal interests isn't just good for your heart and soul, it's good for your wallet too.

Fred Peters learned the hard way that the world of job searching has changed. If you remember from chapter 1, Fred is the director of publications of a major Ivy League university and an avid golfer. Staff cuts and consolidations have taken what was always a stressful position and turned it into a nightmare. Fred decided to be proactive and start getting back in touch with the people in his network and start testing the waters. Based on his study of trade magazines and professional journals, it doesn't seem there are many job openings in higher education. A visit to a meeting of a press group he belonged to resulted in his being overwhelmed with résumés. Apparently, everyone there was already out of work. Telephone calls to other business contacts asking for help in lining up informational interviews have been fruitless. Some people don't even return his calls or e-mails. His mentor, a former manager, admitted to him that he hasn't been able to get interviews for himself, let alone for Fred. To make matters worse, there are rumors that the new president of the university is looking to cut even more staff.

## The Changing Job Search

For years, most job openings were announced simply by putting a Help Wanted or Now Hiring sign in a store, office, or factory window. Even in today's high-tech, sophisticated world it's interesting to see how many businesses still use this traditional technique to find employees. Walk through all but the most economically depressed communities today and you'll see a number of such simple requests for applications.

However, most jobs today are advertised in newspapers and/or magazines. One reason is that only a handful of businesses now have sufficient physical exposure to enough human traffic for those simple window signs to be effective. And, of course, by advertising in publications, businesses can pull from a much larger pool of potential candidates. That's essential if you're looking for people with particular skills and experiences. A beverage-distribution firm looking to hire an experienced wine salesperson fluent in Italian can't count on many such folks walking by their office complex in a suburban industrial park. The fewer people who possess the desired combination of skills and experience, the more mass market the publications need to be for the ads to be effective.

Existing open positions are almost always advertised in one way or another. Even if the job is likely to be filled through an in-house promotion, the position may be advertised if for no other reason than meeting legal obligations. The great advantage of applying for jobs advertised in newspapers and magazines is that you know there's a definite and immediate opening. Someone desperate to generate a stream of income as soon as possible can look to ads for immediate leads. That's something I'll get back to in a later chapter when I discuss what to do if you're currently unemployed. Still, in recent years most of my clients, and I'll wager a great many of you reading this book, have all but ignored help wanted ads. That's because in the past twenty or thirty years it has become accepted wisdom that the best jobs aren't advertised.

I think it was in the 1970s that people began to believe help wanted ads weren't for elite job searchers. There *was* a great deal of truth to this belief. Many times, companies didn't post wanted ads for positions, because they hadn't yet fired the person holding the position. Rather than terminating someone the company felt was underperforming, there would be a discrete private job search. Only after a replacement was found would the current employee be let go. By keeping the potential job opening private a company could also, in effect, test the waters. If it didn't find any candidates more attractive than its current employee, it would bite the bullet and keep him or her . . . at least for the moment. Because filling lower-level jobs is always easier—there are simply more candidates—this backdoor job filling was reserved for positions that were tougher to fill and, which, therefore, paid more. In fact, the harder the job was to fill, and the more it paid, the more likely the whole process would take place privately.

I was let into how this practice worked in the late 1970s, when I got a call from David Zimmer. I had first met David when I was appearing regularly as a television commentator. He was CFO of the network at the time, and he and I had to negotiate some issues. David asked me to serve as his representative in a hush-

hush negotiation. He had been called at home by a headhunter who had been hired by a cable network. The headhunter said the CEO of the other network was looking to replace his own CFO and David was one of the handful of people qualified for the job. But since the CEO wasn't sure he'd be able to steal someone away from another network, he was using the headhunter to approach the candidates discretely and sequentially. The entire process had to be kept secret from the rest of the company and the media. David hired me to be his cutout, and the whole process actually took place between the headhunter and me rather than between David and the CEO.

Sometimes a private job opening was created, not by the company's disappointment, but by a candidate coming forward and offering him- or herself to the company. Let's say a superb graphic artist privately went to an advertising agency and offered her services. The agency, blown away by the individual, decided to make a place for her even if one didn't exist, either by terminating someone it felt was less competent than the new person, or by creating an entirely new position. In the 1970s and 1980s I saw this happen a great deal in very competitive businesses. For example, that graphic designer who approached the ad agency might have been working for a competing ad agency. By hiring her the agency not only helped itself, it hurt a competitor.

This was how Sandra Lustick landed a very lucrative position with a software firm in the 1980s. Sandra had gone to college with one of my daughters. I had helped her purchase an apartment and negotiate a raise with the software firm for which she worked. A couple of years later Sandra came to me with an idea for a new business. We discussed it and realized that there was already a company that could provide the product and service Sandra envisioned. Rather than starting from scratch, I coached Sandra to approach this firm. She put together an excellent proposal about how it could slightly alter one of its products and then potentially take advantage of a huge untapped market. The president of the company was so impressed that he hired Sandra on the spot, excited both by the prospect of a new revenue stream, and by the prospect of stealing a star salesperson away from a competitor.

There were also times these private openings were created through the personal whim of an executive. Maybe the CFO's nephew had just graduated college and hadn't yet found a job. His mother turned to her brother at a weekend barbecue and said something like, "You're a big-shot CFO at Acme Inc. After all I've done for you and your kids over the years, why can't you get my son a job?" The CFO then went to the human resources director the subsequent Monday morning, presented his nephew's résumé, and "asked" if there were any jobs for this dazzling young man. Depending on the clout of the CFO, and yes, the merit of the young man in question, the HR director might have created or forced a place for him.

My client Sara Ciannesco had to make a hire in just these kinds of circumstances. Sara owns two very successful high-end women's clothing stores in Manhattan. One of the well-known designers whose work the store featured heard Sara was looking for a new salesperson for her downtown store. The designer said he had just the person for the job: a young woman who was trying to crack into the world of fashion modeling. It just so happened she was also dating the designer. Sara, needing to remain on good terms with the designer, hired the young lady. While she didn't become a stellar employee, she became adequate, and actually lasted longer as a clothing salesperson than she did as the designer's girlfriend.

As more and more people recognized there was a backdoor job market, as well as the more public job market represented by the help wanted ads, people developed a new job-search approach. Answering ads was no longer enough. You had to network.

## The Age of Networking

The principle behind networking is that the best jobs are filled, not by answering ads, but by making business connections. The idea is to develop a mutually supporting network of individuals with whom you have business relationships. These could be people you worked with, worked for, competed against, partnered with, sold to, or bought from. You meet these people informally, let's say for lunch, and talk about what you are doing and what they are doing. The idea is to create sources of information about those private job openings. The more you network, the more of an insider you become. The quid pro quo is that you too are ready, willing, and able to help others find those private jobs.

Along with their own contacts, ambitious networkers go to events, meetings, conventions, and trade shows, and meet people who might know about some private job openings, or meet people who know other people who know about some private job openings. Even if no immediate private job opening appears, they press the flesh, hand out their business cards, and subtly make it clear that they are in the market for any such openings that might one day appear. Sometimes these networks revolve around industries, other times around professions. Perhaps all the dental hygienists in a city gather regularly for a meeting at which they hear a manufacturer's representative talk about a new piece of equipment, have dinner, complain about dentists, and share inside information on private job openings.

Renatta Kahn was one of my clients who actually turned net-working from a job-search technique into a lifestyle. I helped Renatta when, as a young attorney specializing in entertainment law, she negotiated her contract as an in-house counsel for a large, multifaceted media corporation. Renatta was a single, at-tractive woman in her midthirties with an incredible drive to succeed. Renatta had breakfast with the same three other enter-tainment lawyers every morning at a café in a small boutique hotel. Over coffee and juice in this discreet location they traded inside information and gossip. After work, Renatta's schedule was filled with meetings of a bar association committee on Mondays, drinks at a television industry gathering on Tuesdays, a publishing industry roundtable and dinner on Wednesdays, and a standing dinner date with her boss on Thursdays. She spent almost every weekend with a handful of business guests at a house she owned on the eastern end of Long Island. The only time Renatta didn't seem to be networking was when she jogged, which she did religiously first thing every morning—though I'm sure if she could have found an entertainment in-dustry runners' group, she would have joined.

As networking became more widespread, and as people began to look to move beyond their own industry or profession, a variation de-veloped. This is what I called Rolodex renting, and it involves the use of informational interviews.

You may want to shift to a job in the widget industry. Unfortu-nately, you know only one person in widgets. Rather than relying on social gatherings and your own limited set of contacts, you ask your contacts for help in finding people who might be able help you "learn if the widget industry is right for you." In effect, you rent other people's Rolodexes, asking them to introduce you to any of their own contacts in the widget business. In this way you exponentially increase the reach of an existing network.

Once you get a name, you call, write, or e-mail the individual, asking for an informational interview, dropping the name of the person who referred you. Outwardly you are simply asking to pick the interviewer's brains about the widget business, since it's something you find interesting. Actually you are trying to get him or her to hire you, but saying so would limit the number of people willing to speak with you.

At these informational interviews you do everything you can to impress the heck out of the interviewer and get him or her to give you a job. If that doesn't happen, you simply ask for the names of other people who might be helpful in your fascinating voyage of discovery in the land of widgets. You then call these new names and repeat the process, dropping the name of the person who made the referral.

The interviewers are not necessarily motivated by your being able to help them get a job, since they are probably much higher on the corporate ladder than you; instead, they want to be able to refer their own contacts to the person who referred you. Instead of it being a direct quid pro quo—"I'll help you if you help me"—it is second-degree quid pro quo—"I'll help the person you send me if you help the person I send you."

This process of working your own network, renting other people's Rolodexes, and then going on a series of informational interviews is the method of choice for most people looking for good-paying, mid- to upper-level, white-collar work. Sure, the want ads are still there and actually got a boost from the Internet, but they aren't seen as being either as effective or as sophisticated as the informational interview circuit.

---

## HOW TO ATTRACT HEADHUNTERS

Because corporate executives are pretty much obsessed with filling upper-level jobs only by employee-jacking, and human resources departments have effectively put an end to informational interviews, headhunters will remain the only route to the upper levels of a company. How do you show up on their radar screens?

Make sure you're still working. No matter what they may say, headhunters are hired in order to poach employees from competitors.

Forget about contacting them and presenting yourself as a potential candidate. The headhunter motto is "Don't call us, we'll call you." Remember, they're not looking to find jobs for people, they're looking to find people for jobs.

Instead, become an informant for them. Tell them you're interested in developing a relationship and then offer up everything you know about your company. Give them enough names, titles, phone numbers, and e-mail addresses to compile an organizational chart and directory of your company. Headhunters believe in a quid pro quo, but want their quid up front.

---

But in the past couple of years this circuit has run out of power. Since the bursting of the Internet bubble, the terrorist attacks of September 11, and the subsequent recession, it has been getting more and more difficult for people to find anyone willing to give them an informational interview. I have to admit I've stopped giving them myself. That's because it's obvious to everyone now that these are nothing more than job interviews in disguise. With so many people requesting informational interviews, and with so few actual job openings, it has become time-consuming and ultimately fruitless to give these interviews.

Human resources departments have successfully fought against filling positions through networking. All those behind-the-scenes interviews and meetings threatened their existence. Why have a personnel department if you weren't going to use it to find and screen candidates? In order to provide the secrecy many executives sought, the HR people took to hiring headhunters (often former HR people themselves) to do the screening of potential candidates. (See the box on page 133: How to Attract Headhunters.)

## Make It Personal

One of the themes I keep coming back to in this book is that merit isn't enough to succeed at work anymore. It's also not enough to get a foot in the door these days. I hate to say it, but in today's job market it's not what you know, but who you know. To get the multiple job offers you're looking for in your job-fishing efforts, you'll need to draw on personal relationships.

Let's say there's a job opening in your department. Your sister has been out of work for about six months, relying on her husband's income and help from your parents to make ends meet. She's qualified for the job . . . but so are the two dozen people represented by the file folder of résumés sitting on your desk. Do you tell your sister about the job and also do everything you can to help her get it, or do you simply treat her like every other candidate? Of course you bend over backward to help your sister get the job.

It's human nature to give preference to those closest to you. That's just accentuated when times are hard, as they are in the job market today. The people making the decisions on whom to meet with, whom to interview, and whom to hire naturally give preference to individuals with whom they have personal relationships. For example, during one of the last major economic downturns in New York a good friend of mine who was a part-time professor and actor was having a hard time making ends meet. I needed help in my office with general office chores and deliveries. Rather than hiring someone with experience, I offered the job to my out-of-work friend. I chose to hire based on personal connection rather than competence. I don't think that's unusual. That's why I think the key to getting jobs in today's work environment is to expand your personal network rather than your business network, and use the former not the latter to generate job leads.

## "That's Terribly Cynical"

Some of my clients balk when I first tell them to expand their personal network and use it to generate job leads. "That's terribly cynical," they say. "At least when you do business networking the quid pro quo is overt. Developing friendships just for business reasons seems dishonest." They're partly right. Developing friendships for business reasons is amoral, if not immoral. But that's not what I'm suggesting at all.

I don't think you should choose your personal relationships with an eye toward their business potential. In fact, I'd suggest you avoid that. Instead, I think you should pursue your true interests. (See the box on page 136: Inventory Your Interests.) Join clubs focusing on a pastime you enjoy, not one that has lots of CEOs as members. Pursue hobbies that will bring you joy, not those you think will bring you affluent chums. Become friendly with people whose company you enjoy, who share your values, who make you laugh. If your efforts at expanding your personal networks are phony you'll get neither personal satisfaction nor job leads. That's because you'll never actually make the kind of personal ties you need. If you're just showing up at the chess club simply because you think you'll get job leads there, your ploy will soon

## INVENTORY YOUR INTERESTS

If you're at a loss for how to develop or expand a personal network, do an inventory of your interests.

What do you like to read? Check with your local bookstores and libraries to see if there's a reading group that caters to that type of book. Do an online search for your favorite authors or genres and see if you can find local or regional fan groups.

What type of entertainment do you like? If you love the movies, check to see if there's a film forum or film society in your community. Fans of popular music should explore the local music scene for folk, rock, jazz, and blues clubs. Classical music aficionados should check for orchestras, chamber groups, or opera companies.

Do you have a talent? Singers should investigate community choirs. Dancers should look for classes or troupes, as well as clubs that have regular events. Artists should go to nearby galleries and art-supply stores and check the bulletin boards. Photographers should go to camera stores, musicians to music stores, and crafters to craft stores. Writers should check bookstores for information on writers groups.

Are you a sports fan? Look for fan clubs online or at the facility where the team plays. Like to play a sport? Look at the bulletin boards in sporting-good shops and check at facilities catering to the sport.

Do you have a hobby? There are lots of hobbyist organizations which that sponsor local chapters. Check online, at hobby shops, or in special-interest magazines. If you haven't pursued a hobby for years, consider picking up one you abandoned when you were younger.

Interested in a particular issue or cause? Get involved in the local political committee of a party of your choice. Volunteer at an organization or institution whose mission you support.

Attend religious services or meeting at the house of worship of your choice. If you're nervous about meeting strangers, religious services are an excellent way to break the ice. People will go out of their way to be welcoming.

be obvious to everyone. Join the chess club because you love chess, and let the job leads develop naturally.

Believe me, leads will develop from your expanded personal network. Become active in a church. Go to the gym and take classes or take part in a sports league. Seek out clubs for those who share your hobbies. Pick up the instrument you set aside after college. Learn a foreign language. Take cooking classes. Form a book group. Volunteer for a local charitable organization or institution.

By expanding your personal network you will meet and develop relationships with a much wider range of people than if your only interactions are with an alumni group, a professional association, and a business organization. Your personal network will include people from different ethnic groups, religions, communities, economic levels, professions, and industries. Because this personal network includes a wider range of people, it offers you access to more possible job leads. And because your links with these individuals will be personal ones, the leads that do develop will be more powerful and more likely to actually result in a job offer.

David Greenstein's networking had run out of steam by the time he came to see me. A thirty-two-year-old reference librarian working at one of the larger branches of a big-city public library system, David had recently received his master's degree in information-system management. While he believed an information professional like himself was exactly what corporate IT departments needed, he had been unable to land any interviews or meetings other than with other public library systems and a couple of university libraries. I suggested he focus on expanding his personal network instead. Since one of David's interests was politics, he decided to get involved in the mayoral campaign of an independent candidate in the suburb in which he lived. One of the chief fund-raisers for the campaign was an older woman who ran a charitable foundation launched years earlier by a media entrepreneur. On election night she and David chatted and celebrated their candidate's victory. They arranged to have lunch together the next week. Within a month of that lunch David was assuming the newly created position of information architect for the foundation.

## "But Won't It Take Too Long?"

Another objection clients sometimes voice to my idea of expanding and using personal networks to generate job leads is that it will take too long. There's some truth to this point as well.

I readily admit that the downside to using your personal network to generate job leads is that those leads, while of a wider range and more powerful, will be slower to develop. While there are instances of love at first sight, and times when people strike up lifelong friendships quickly, it usually takes time for meaningful personal bonds to form. Business networking, on the other hand, is quicker to generate leads because its sole purpose is mutual self-interest. All that's needed for a business relationship to develop is for the two parties to think they can be of some benefit to each other.

However, in today's job market all business networking does is generate poor leads quickly. The speed of the process doesn't matter, since so little is actually coming from most networking today. In addition, there is a way you can speed up at least part of the process.

As I wrote earlier, and will get back to in more detail in a subsequent chapter, answering classified ads and contacting employment agencies is the single best way to get a job—any job—in the short

---

## HOW TO FIND TEMPORARY RELIEF

Signing up with a temporary employment agency is one of the best ways I know to quickly generate a stream of income. The days when temps were nothing more than replacement or emergency file clerks and administrative assistants are over. Today there are temp agencies representing every profession from attorney to xylophone player. In an effort to downsize and save cash, many larger firms have replaced full-time workers who provided support functions with either small service firms or temps. Others, trying to deal with a rapidly changing economy, respond to boosts in business by hiring temps rather than adding staff. Signing up with a temp agency offers a number of advantages. Some provide a better benefits package to their people than would be provided by many full-time employers. Temp agencies offer employees greater flexibility than full-time employers, allowing more freedom to do job fishing. Being a temp is one of the quickest ways to expand knowledge of different industries. And most important, it's easier to get reemployed through a temp agency than on your own.

---

term. (See the box above: How to Find Temporary Relief.) If you need to bring in a stream of income as soon as possible I suggest you use these traditional techniques, and continue trying to generate leads through your business network, at the same time as you expand your personal network. The idea is to get enough income coming in so you can give your personal network the time it needs to generate potentially better job leads and offers.

Don't worry about this being time-consuming. Remember, you will be doing things you enjoy to expand your personal network. These won't be chores, they'll be pleasures. In fact, these are just the things you've always wanted to have the time to do. Now you're making the time for them and getting both personal and professional advantages from it.

> Erin Corbet knew moving from New York City to a small community upstate would complicate her work life. A pastry chef by profession, she was moving because her life partner had landed a tenure-track position at a college upstate. Erin and I worked out a job-fishing plan prior to her move. A week after moving into their new home, Erin answered a classified ad in the local newspaper and landed a job in the bakery department of an upscale supermarket. It was a far cry from the Upper East Side restaurant where she used to work, but it helped pay the bills. Slowly but surely Erin and her partner wove together a social network over the course of a year. At a potluck dinner fund-raiser for a local women's shelter, she met the former owner of a local bistro who was looking to start a new catering business. She hired Erin a week later.

## "I Don't Remember How to Make Friends"

The most surprising objection I've heard from clients about my suggestion to expand their personal network was from Jeanie Murrow, a forty-three-year-old attorney who had been out of the job market for six years during which she was home caring for her daughter. "I don't remember how to make friends," Jeanie said to me. "For the past six years I've focused on my daughter's social life, not my own. Before that everyone I met was an attorney, so all we talked about was the law or legal problems." At first I thought Jeanie's fear was unique to her. But then I heard variations on the same theme from other clients. I realized many people have so compartmentalized their lives that they'd either never learned, or had forgotten, how to socialize in social rather than business situations.

Entering a social situation where you don't know anyone can be intimidating. But once you become comfortable wielding some very simple social skills you'll be able to strike up friendships in almost any setting.

Make sure you have an open, inquisitive mind about meeting new people. Leave your stereotypes at home. Don't think of people in terms of their professions, or their appearance, or their ethnic group. Treat everyone as potentially interesting and a possible future friend. The thirty-something millionaire software executive could be a selfish bore who does nothing for you, while the sixty-something barber could be a fascinating individual who provides just the connection you need.

## Appearance Counts

While you shouldn't make judgments about the appearance of others, take some care with your own. Appropriateness is what counts in social settings, not fashion. You should be wearing something that is clean and that fits the occasion.

More important than your clothing is your expression and manner. There is no single better way to make friends than to smile when you say hello. Look people in the eye when you're introduced, give a firm but not obnoxious handshake, and repeat their first name back to them. (This is, after all, a social setting, so first names are fine.) For example, when someone says, "Hello, I'm Mark Levine," you respond by saying, "Hello, Mark, I'm Stephen Pollan, it's nice to meet you."

## Engaging with Strangers

Ask questions. Everyone has a story to tell, and most people enjoy talking about themselves. Try to frame your questions so they can't be answered with just a yes or a no. When he or she starts to answer, listen closely and don't interrupt. Look the other person in the eye and smile while he or she is talking to you. Nod every so often, and use verbal cues of support like "I see," "yes," "oh really," and even "uh-huh." When the other person stops talking, ask one further question to clarify what he or she has been saying. Any more than that and it will seem like an interrogation rather than a conversation. Don't argue or disagree. It's better to react a beat slow and make sure you're laughing with someone rather than laughing at him or her. Avoid frowning or showing any outward signs you doubt what he or she is saying. Say you can identify with what is being said, but don't turn the conversation to you. That will seem like you're trying to outdo or one-up the other person.

If you can't draw the other person out by asking about him or her, talk about something you share. That could be a mutual interest, such as what brings both to the occasion, or it could be something in the news. It's better to talk about the weather than religion or politics, even if you're in a religious or political setting.

By this point, any polite social person will return your sign of being interested in him or her by asking about you. Take your cue as to how long to talk and how much detail to reveal from his or her answers to your questions. If possible, point out similarities between you and the other person. For example, you could say, "Like you and your wife, I'm new to town." Again, make sure you don't one-up the other person while pointing out similarities. Talk about your current job and future job plans and goals, but don't dwell on work issues. People will want to know what you do, but they'll also want to know who you are. You want them to like you and to want to help you because of their personal connection to you, not because of the company for which you work or the profession you practice.

If the other party doesn't ask you about yourself, or if he or she doesn't look you in the eye when talking, feel free to politely excuse yourself and break off the conversation. There's no need to find an excuse with such people, since they're clearly not interested in speaking with you. Simply offer your hand and say, "I'm glad we met." Then move off to chat with someone else.

## Cultivating Friendships

Having made a terrific first impression, you should do all you can to keep it up at subsequent social gatherings. Make sure you're always polite, saying "please," "may I," "thank you," and "you're welcome." It's better to appear overly polite than boorish. Pay attention to details and praise people whenever you can. People like to know that the little things they do are noticed and appreciated by others. Continue to treat everyone as being important.

Offer help whenever it appears needed and don't sulk if others fail to respond in kind immediately. But don't rush to make promises or to take on tasks that you may not be able to keep or do in an effort to ingratiate. That smacks of desperation and only leads to mutual disappointment. Instead, pick your spots and make sure you deliver on your promises. You want to be known as someone who does what he says he's going to do, not someone who tries to do everything.

Finally, make sure that while you're cultivating friends you're not also making enemies. Don't engage in backstabbing or gossip. However, you don't need to criticize it either. Simply don't get into the conversation. If forced to say something, offer up a noncommittal statement like "I really don't know him that well" or "I haven't really thought about it." Remain neutral in feuds and avoid petty politics—there's enough of that at work. In a social setting you should have only friends, acquaintances, and people you don't know.

The more often you speak with someone, the more detail of your work situation you can feel free to reveal. There will be some people who will feel a kinship with you right away and will try to help you find job offers. There will be others for whom it takes a bit of time to feel comfortable endorsing you to third parties. Continue to be a warm, caring individual and eventually they'll come around.

There will also be some people who, while establishing a friendship with you, never extend the offer of assistance with your work life. Some people are uncomfortable talking about money or work, or mixing their social and work lives to any extent. Getting to know them isn't a wasted effort, though. You can never have too many friends. And as long as they contribute something to your life, they're well worth having. You never know where friendships will lead.

## Fred Peters Expands His Social Network

I received a telephone call from Fred Peters after he'd realized his networking was going nowhere and no one was eager to give him an informational interview. We met for an hour, and I told him about my concept of expanding his personal network and using it as a source of job leads. Fred, a very affable, warm individual, was perfectly suited to this strategy.

An avid golfer, Fred joined a second foursome and began spending more time at the clubhouse both before and after his rounds of golf. One of Fred's son was active in a youth hockey league, and after years of being only peripherally active in the youth hockey organization, Fred volunteered to join the board. During college and for a short time after graduation, Fred had been active in amateur theater. He decided to return to that interest and got involved in a small local theater company. To help him get his "acting chops" back, he signed up for an improvisation class given by a local community college. Meanwhile, Fred kept an eye on the want ads and tried to stay in touch with his business network.

While he was able to navigate successfully the changes made by the incoming university president, Fred didn't let that temporary respite deter his job fishing. One afternoon after a round of golf Fred struck up a conversation with a guest of one of the fellows in his regular foursome. It turned out that, like Fred, the guest was a Cincinnati native. They had gone to neighboring high schools, though a few years apart. They also shared painful memories of being Bengals and Reds fans.

About six weeks later they met at the club again. It turned out that the fellow had been in town for a job interview before and had just taken a job as general manager of a large printing firm headquartered nearby. He told Fred he had been brought in by the printing firm's parent company to update and upgrade the operation. Fred spoke to him about his experiences integrating new technology into the university's publications program. They had a follow-up meeting for lunch. A month later Fred was offered the job of assistant general manager of the firm, in charge of modernizing the prepress arm of the business.

I know it's ironic that while on the one hand I preach separating your work and personal life by looking to one for money and the other for satisfaction, on the other hand I advocate using your social life to generate job leads. It's also ironic that I've found my clients get far more job leads by *not* making that the priority in their social life than if it's obvious they're using a social setting to find a job. It has taken me a long time to accept these kinds of inconsistencies in the way the work world appears to function.

I take comfort in Ralph Waldo Emerson's aphorism that a foolish consistency is the hobgoblin of little minds. I know what I'm suggesting can seem ironic and counterintuitive. But what matters is that it works.

One element of my approach that *isn't* counterintuitive is that if you're looking at work as a way to generate money, you've got to make money a priority. Putting money first is the subject of the next chapter.

# CHAPTER 7

# It's the Money

*Work though we must, our jobs do not automatically
determine our priorities concerning our marriages, our
children, our social life, or even our health. It's still life,
constrained as it may be by limited disposable income or
leisure time, and we're still responsible for making it
something we enjoy or endure.*

—MELINDA M. MARSHALL

THE FIRST SURPRISE for Will Sykes was that his job fishing actually worked. He found himself weighing two job offers simultaneously. A lieutenant in the police force of a small city in the New York suburbs, Will was offered a job as director of security at a television studio as well as a job as assistant director of security at an aviation industry facility. Will's second surprise was that, after weighing the two jobs, he chose the one at the industrial facility. The studio job offered more amenities, more of a challenge, a better title, chances for advancement, and a great deal of status. But the industrial job was closer to his home and paid a bit more. And when weighing job offers today, Will realized he had to focus on financial issues.

Look for emotional, psychological, and spiritual fulfillment in your personal life, and you won't need to choose jobs that offer psychic rewards at the expense of material rewards.

Work to live rather than live to work, and you won't need to choose jobs that make your working hours more comfortable. Instead, you can focus on factors that give you more time at home.

Accept that your route to advancement is through changing jobs rather than climbing a ladder, and you'll see chances for personal development are more valuable than chances to move up in the company.

Follow the fire-your-boss philosophy and your priorities will shift dramatically.

Fabulous amenities and a supportive culture won't be as important as more paid personal and vacation days.

A great work environment won't carry the same weight as being closer to your home.

And an impressive title and lots of status simply won't compare to a better salary.

Today, when it comes to analyzing which job offer to accept and which to reject, you need to remember the sixth element in my work philosophy: it's the money that matters.

That's what I had to explain to Debbie O'Leary when she came into my office for the first time. If you recall from chapter 1, Debbie was a program director at a midwestern rock radio station. She moved to New York City in order to be with her new husband, Bruce, a well-known deejay at one of the city's premier rock stations. Debbie had never had any problem with paying her dues and working her way up the ladder during her twenty years in radio. But she had always worked at rock stations and had always had her own show. It was love of rock music that had drawn her to radio in the first place, and it was the thrill of being on the air that kept her in the business through the many lean times. And moving back to New York, where she had been raised, led to another of those lean times. It took more than eighteen months for Debbie to find any potential jobs; then, as fate would have it, she received two offers: one as a part-time weekend replacement deejay at one of the city's rock stations, and the other as a jazz programmer at a satellite radio network. Her reflexive reaction was to take the job at the rock station, but Bruce urged her to come see me before making her decision.

## Isolating the Twenty Factors

Whenever most people are faced with having to choose between two alternate courses or paths, they make a list of the characteristics of each option. Let's say you're trying to decide where to go for dinner. One choice is the local diner, the other is a French restaurant. If you're like most of us, you mentally go through a checklist of the factors that enter into your decision making. The French restaurant has a more pleasant environment and the food is more substantial, albeit specialized. The diner is less expensive, closer to your home, and offers more choices.

The same holds true for choosing between job offers. The first step in the process is to make a list of the characteristics of each job, based on a set of factors. Over years of consulting and helping people weigh job offers, I've found there are twenty main factors people consider. Here they are in alphabetical order:

1. Amenities: services provided by the organization for your use at no or very low cost.

2. Auto: a car and its associated expenses provided for you at no charge by the organization.

3. Challenging: the degree to which the job provides you with intellectual stimulation.

4. Culture: the beliefs, customs, practices, and values of the organization as a whole and the specific department of which you'd be a part.

5. Disability insurance: a policy that pays a benefit if you become disabled, paid for by the organization.

6. Environment: the comfort and aesthetics of both the general and your specific work spaces.

7. Expense allowance: a regularly provided stipend given to you for business-related expenses.

8. Health insurance: a policy covering all or part of the cost of medical, dental, pharmaceutical, psychological, and lifestyle counseling services, paid for entirely, or in part, by the organization.

9. Income: how much money you're paid in wages, salary, or bonuses.

10. Life insurance: a policy that pays a benefit on your death, to beneficiaries you select, paid for by the organization.

11. Opportunity for advancement: the potential for your moving up the organization's hierarchy.

12. Opportunity for learning: the potential for you to acquire new skills and knowledge.

13. Paid time off: how many days you can take off work for vacation or personal reasons and still be paid.

14. Proximity: the distance or time required to get from your home to the job and back.

15. Retirement plan: an investment or pension plan that the organization sets up and to which it may contribute.

16. Stability: the relative security of the company or organization because of its established nature and its long-standing role in an industry.

17. Status: the relative standing of the job in your industry, community, or some other group.

18. Title: the value of the descriptive name for the job you'd hold.

19. Tuition reimbursement: a stipend to pay the cost of further education that may or may not be specifically related to your job.

20. Unpaid time off: the opportunity for you to take time off work for professional or personal reasons and not hurt your job status.

## Charting the Factors for Job Offers

I've always found that writing things down helps focus decision making. Nowhere is that more true than in weighing competing job offers. Take out that pad you used for all your early exercises and during your job fishing. Turn to a fresh page and divide it into columns that represent one more than the number of job offers you're weighing. In other words, if you have two offers to choose between, divide the page into three columns; if you have three offers, divide the page into four columns.

Label the first column Factors. Label the remaining columns with

## COMPARING JOB OFFERS

| FACTOR | OFFER #1 | OFFER #2 |
|---|---|---|
| Amenities | | |
| Auto | | |
| Challenging | | |
| Culture | | |
| Disability insurance | | |
| Environment | | |
| Expense allowance | | |
| Health insurance | | |
| Income | | |
| Life insurance | | |
| Opportunity for advancement | | |
| Opportunity for learning | | |
| Paid time off | | |
| Proximity | | |
| Retirement plan | | |
| Stability | | |
| Status | | |
| Title | | |
| Tuition reimbursement | | |
| Unpaid time off | | |

a word or phrase that describes each job offer. For example, if you've received two offers and one is an offer from a telecommunications company and the other is from a medical-research firm you might label the second column Telecom and the third Medical.

Go back to the first column, and move down the page writing a word or phrase that corresponds to each of the twenty factors, each on its own line. Skip one or two spaces between each item. If you need to jump to a second page, just replicate the columns and their headings on the new page.

(While I'd prefer you invest a bit in the process and create your own chart, in the interests of convenience I've also provided a blank form on page 152 that you could also use for this purpose. But I'd suggest that, rather than filling in this form in the book, you photocopy it and work on the photocopy instead. After all, you're going to have so many offers coming in now that you've started job fishing that you won't want to use up the chart on your first pair of offers.)

Now, fill in details about each factor for each offer. For instance, if the Telecom job offer includes a company gym, write "gym" on the amenities line in the Telecom column. If the Medical job offer includes free use of a company cafeteria, write "meals" on the amenities line in the Medical column. Go down the list, providing as much information as you can about each offer.

After you've filled in all the blanks, consider each line individually. Which of the two job offers seems to provide the better deal in each factor? Does the Telecom job offer two weeks' paid vacation, while the Medical job offer provides three? Advantage Medical. Is the Telecom job located thirty minutes from your home while the Medical job is located sixty minutes away? Advantage Telecom. Place a large check mark on each line in the column of the job that provides the better deal.

## Debbie O'Leary Charts the Factors for
## Her Two Job Offers

After sitting with me for a about an hour, Debbie agreed not to react reflexively and instead compare the two job offers she'd received. If you recall, one was for a part-time deejay position at a rock station, and the other was for a jazz programming position at a satellite radio network. Using a legal pad, she drew up the chart I recommended in order to break each offer down into the twenty factors I'd outlined. (See the box on page 155: Debbie O'Leary's Offer Comparison Chart.)

*Amenities.* The deejay position at the radio station offered no amenities. The satellite radio station gave employees a discounted rate at a health club located near its offices. Advantage: Satellite.

*Auto.* Neither job offered a company car, but the radio station would pay car expenses if Debbie had to travel to a remote location for a broadcast. Advantage: Radio.

*Challenging.* Because Debbie had been a rock deejay for her entire working life, the radio job offered no challenges for her. The satellite radio job presented a challenge because it meant Debbie would need to come up with playlists in a new genre and format. Advantage: Satellite.

*Culture.* The bohemian, free-spirited culture of the radio station was one that Debbie adored, having been part of similar cultures in the past. The satellite radio job, on the other hand, had a much more corporate culture. Advantage: Radio.

*Disability insurance.* Neither job offered disability insurance. No advantage.

*Environment.* The radio station's studio was located in a somewhat run-down old office building in midtown Manhattan. The satellite radio company was located in a brand-new facility in a corporate park in suburban New Jersey. Advantage: Satellite.

## DEBBIE O'LEARY'S OFFER COMPARISON CHART

| FACTOR | RADIO | SATELLITE |
|---|---|---|
| Amenities | none | health club discount √ |
| Auto | none | none |
| Challenging | no √ | yes √ |
| Culture | bohemian | corporate |
| Disability insurance | no | no |
| Environment | run-down office building | new, modern facility √ |
| Expense allowance | no | no |
| Health insurance | not as p/t | yes √ |
| Income | 30K | 75K √ |
| Life insurance | no | no |
| Opportunity for advancement | yes | no |
| Opportunity for learning | no | yes √ |
| Paid time off | no | 2 weeks plus 4 days √ |
| Proximity | 30 minutes each way √ | 45 minutes each way |
| Retirement plan | not for p/t | 401 (k) w/$ match √ |
| Stability | yes, for radio √ | no, start-up |
| Status | high status √ | no status |
| Title | no value | some value √ |
| Tuition reimbursement | none | none |
| Unpaid time off | great deal √ | 10 days parental leave |

*Expense allowance*. Neither job offered an expense allowance. No advantage.

*Health insurance*. The radio station did not provide health coverage for part-time employees until they worked for the company for more than two years. The satellite radio company offered a complete health insurance package. Advantage: Satellite.

*Income*. Because Debbie was a member of the union she would earn approximately $30,000 a year as a part-time deejay at the radio station. The full-time satellite radio job offered a salary of $75,000. Advantage: Satellite.

*Life insurance*. Neither job offered life insurance. No advantage.

*Opportunity for advancement*. The radio job gave Debbie the chance to move eventually into a full-time deejay job with a regular air shift. The structure of the satellite radio company seemed to provide little chance for upward movement for programmers. Instead, there would be lateral movement to other genres. Advantage: Radio.

*Opportunity for learning*. Debbie could do the radio job in her sleep. The satellite job would require her to learn the dynamics of a new segment of the radio business, and a new musical genre. Advantage: Satellite.

*Paid time off*. The radio job gave no paid vacation or personal days to part-timers. As a fill-in, Debbie would probably be working many if not all holidays. The satellite job offered two weeks' paid vacation and four paid personal days each year. Advantage: Satellite.

*Proximity*. The radio job was a thirty-minute subway ride each way from Debbie's apartment. The satellite job was a forty-five minute combined subway and commuter train trip each way. Advantage: Radio.

*Retirement plan*. The radio station had no retirement plan for part-timers. The satellite job offered a 401(k) plan and matched annual contributions up to a certain amount. Advantage: Satellite.

*Stability*. While radio wasn't a secure industry, the station where

Debbie would be working had been one of the two top FM rock radio stations in the New York market for more than a decade. The satellite radio company was a start-up in a new industry. Advantage: Radio.

*Status.* Being a programmer for a satellite radio network didn't have anywhere near the status of being an on-air personality in America's largest media market. Advantage: Radio.

*Title.* The title of deejay carried no particular weight—what mattered were the size of the market and the ratings. Program director was a more advanced title in the business, implying a step up the management hierarchy. Advantage: Satellite.

*Tuition reimbursement.* Neither job offered tuition reimbursement. No advantage.

*Unpaid time off.* Because it was a part-time job, the deejay position didn't provide lots of unpaid time off. The satellite job offered ten days' unpaid parental leave. Advantage: Radio.

Analyzing the offers in this manner convinced Debbie her husband and I were probably right in discouraging her from reflexively grabbing the deejay job. However, it also showed neither job offer was perfect.

## Setting Priorities

Debbie's realization that neither job was perfect shouldn't have come as a shock. No job is going to be perfect and offer the best of all these factors. It's also unlikely any one job will offer clear advantages over another job in every single one of these categories. If it did there really wouldn't be a choice; it would be obvious which was better. In order to weigh the offers you'll be receiving because of your successful job fishing, you need to prioritize these factors.

Let's go back to our going-out-to-dinner scenario. Both choices—

the local diner and the French restaurant—have their advantages, so you need to prioritize the factors involved to make your choice. If spending less money, for instance, is a priority, you'll opt for the diner. If, on the other hand, having a relaxing dining experience is your priority, the French restaurant will be your choice. You need to go through a similar process when it comes to choosing between job offers. The problem is that many of my clients, and I'm afraid many of you, seem to spend as little time determining their priorities in choosing one job offer over another as in deciding whether to go to the diner or the French restaurant.

Just as we've let false idealism cloud our eyes as to the purpose work should serve in our lives, we've let it cloud our eyes as to what our priorities should be in choosing one job offer over another. If you continue to believe work is an end in itself, and that the psychological rewards you receive from it are more important than any material rewards, you're going to place a priority on those factors that seem to offer psychological value. On the other hand, if you accept, as I've been urging, that work is simply a means to an end, and that therefore the material rewards it offers are the most valuable, you'll place priority on an entirely different set of factors. Since you'll be getting emotional, psychological, and spiritual rewards from your personal life, you won't need to get them from your work life, and as a result, some of the factors that used to loom large should no longer matter as much.

And just as we've let others determine our work futures, we've let them convince us what our priorities should be. It's the role of a company to be as profitable as possible. Part of its effort to maximize profits is to increase efficiency. While there are lots of ways to do that, the most common is to get as much work from employees as possible, while paying them as little as possible. In that effort, companies have worked hard to offer "psychic" as opposed to financial rewards to employees, knowing that doing so is in the company's best interest. For instance, it costs nothing to give an employee a fancy title, but giving him a raise impacts the bottom line. Similarly, companies do everything they can to get employees to work longer hours without paying more money. Some simply issue threats, covertly or overtly, saying the extended hours are a requirement for keeping your job. Others are more subtle and sophisticated, and try to make the workplace as much like home as possible and coming in early and staying late at the job as convenient as possible. These efforts fit neatly into the mind-set that you live to work, and that your identity is wrapped up in your job. Abandon those notions and these efforts lose their power over you.

## Factors That Are No Longer Important

Whenever I go over the list of factors that I believe are no longer important in selecting one job offer over another, my clients' jaws drop. That's because, as you'll see, many of these unimportant factors are exactly those that are most touted by employers and employees alike as being what makes a wonderful place to work. That proves my point. I think it's more important for home to be a wonderful place to live than for your job to be a wonderful place to work.

*Amenities.* I'm always amazed at the extent to which some companies will go to bring their employees in early and keep them there late. Company gyms, cafeterias, and day-care centers are all terrific for people who want to spend most of their lives in the office or at the plant. But you want to spend as much time at home as you can. As a result, these amenities will actually interfere with your goals. The same goes for the concierge-type services being offered by cutting-edge firms today. If the company will pick up your dry cleaning and prescriptions for you, you'll end up staying later than you should. Remember: the goal is to separate your work and your personal lives, not blur them into one. Whenever there's a blurring of that line, work wins out over life.

*Auto.* Company cars benefit the company, not the employee. They are issued only when it makes more financial sense for the company to lease a fleet of vehicles than to reimburse employees for use of their own vehicles. Using your own car for work needn't be a burden. Auto leases allow people to obtain use of late-model cars for less money than it costs to buy them. Expenses incurred by the business use of your car that aren't reimbursed by your employer can be used as a deduction on your income tax return. The only purpose served by your getting a company car is that it makes you feel more important and valued.

*Challenging.* I get a lot of reflexive resistance from clients when I tell them a job's being challenging isn't an important factor. "But it's important to me to be challenged," is the usual first response. Followed by, "If I'm going to be working long hours I'll need to be motivated." I agree it's important to have challenges in life . . . but they don't need to come from work. God knows raising a child is a challenge. So is renovating a bathroom. Hiking the Appalachian Trail is a physical challenge . . . and reading James Joyce is an intellectual one. Thinking your challenges must come from work is indicative of old-style thinking. Stop living to work and start working to live. Similarly, you don't need challenges to keep all those hours at work interesting, because you won't be spending all those hours at work anymore. By focusing on helping your boss meet his or her needs you'll earn the freedom to spend less time at work and more time at home . . . where you'll find all the really rewarding challenges in life.

*Culture.* I'll admit that, all other things being equal, it would be better to work for a company of whose values you approve. But it certainly should not be a deciding factor in choosing one job over another. Placing a high priority on a company's culture says to me that you're still viewing yourself as an employee first and an individual second. There are horrible people who work for Ben & Jerry's and wonderful people who work for Philip Morris. And there are wonderful people at Ben & Jerry's and horrible people at Philip Morris. Where people choose to work has no bearing on what type of people they are. I'd suggest you don't get wrapped up arguing corporate morality either. Philip Morris does make products that can give people cancer. But Ben & Jerry's makes products that can make people obese, which could lead to fatal heart attacks. As long as you're doing honest work it doesn't matter for whom you do it. The place to express your values is in your personal life. Lead a good life, that's what matters. There's nothing contradictory about working at Anheuser-Busch and being an active member of Mothers Against Drunk Driving. You are not your job and your job is not you.

*Environment.* The only environmental issue I think should enter into your decision-making process when choosing one job offer over another is safety. If your life will be in danger at one of the workplaces under consideration, scratch it off your list. Otherwise you should ignore your surroundings. Don't get me wrong: it's nicer to work in a lovely bright private office with windows overlooking a magnificent mountain range than in a dark interior cubicle piled high with boxes. But that shouldn't be a factor in your choice. Employers create pleasant work environments, not out of the goodness of their hearts but because they think it will keep you at your desk longer and/or improve your work. The more homelike your workplace, the more time you'll spend there. I believe the opposite is true as well. The more businesslike your workplace, the less time you'll work there and the more time you'll spend at home. That's why I encourage my clients not to personalize their work spaces. I don't think you should have anything in your work space that you couldn't carry home with you in your briefcase or shoulder bag at the end of the day. Resist the urge to put down psychological or physical roots in the workplace. I've actually encouraged clients who were long-term employees at a prior employer to bring every trace of themselves home every night—packing up the family photo on their desk and their coffee cup. I'm trying to reinforce that a workplace isn't a haven and it shouldn't be a home.

*Expense allowance.* I've never understood clients who viewed expense allowances as a positive factor in a job offer. The two most common allowances I've run across in my practice are companies that offer their outside salespeople a certain amount each month as an automobile allowance, and media companies that offer their executives a monthly stipend for clothing. For some reason, clients see these as being bonuses piled on top of their salary. In reality, I think they're indicative of an employer's efforts to control an employee's life. The employer is saying you can have this money as long as you spend it on something of which I approve and that benefits the company. If it's important for you to have a car for business, and the company is willing to spend, say, $500 a month on an auto allowance, it should simply add that $500 into your monthly salary and leave it to you to decide how much you need to spend on transportation. So, far from being important positive factors, I see expense allowances as warning signs of controlling employers.

*Opportunities for advancement.* This is the factor employers love to tout to young people as an inducement to accept a job that offers a low salary. It's ironic that they use the most outdated rationalization to sway the youngest candidates. But that's because students don't yet know how the real world works. They move up each year simply by doing satisfactory work, and they think the real world works like education. A job that offered "room to move up" was indeed a good thing . . . back when people actually moved up in an organization. But for more than two decades the people who have stepped into those higher spots have come from outside the organization. As I noted earlier in the book, the average thirty-two-year-old American has already worked for nine different firms. That's because there is no upward movement from within anymore. It's a catch-22: stick around long enough to be a candidate for upward mobility and you're marked as being somehow deficient . . . for sticking around that long. Today, opportunities for advancement are actually just opportunities to learn how to please new bosses. I warn my more experienced clients who occasionally hear this pitch not to think they've stumbled onto the one company in America that still believes in promoting from within. It's a lie. To move up you must move out.

*Stability.* In times of economic upheaval many people think the perceived stability of a potential employer is an important factor in weighing job offers. Actually, I think it's a mistake to attach any significance to a company's stability. Whenever a client cites stability as being important, I ask her to give me an example of a stable company. Then I give her a quick homework assignment, asking her to do an online search combining the name of that company and the word "layoffs." Of course, a host of articles and links will appear showing how many thousands, or tens of thousands, the company has let go in the past few years. That's because there's really no such thing as a stable company anymore. Large firms are trying to act small. Small firms are trying to look large. And every firm seems obsessed with its value, as expressed by its share price, rather than its profits. The quickest and surest way to boost the value of your shares is to lay people off. Giant conglomerates change their names repeatedly to reflect the relative share values of their merged components. Relying on the perceived stability of a potential employer is counting on lottery winnings to serve as your retirement plan. Sure, it's remotely possible, but the odds are against you. Yes, the "stable" company may still exist in ten years, but its entire staff may have turned over five times in that period.

*Status.* Let me go back and again ask an important question from earlier in this book: why are you working? If you're working to impress other people, to please your parents, or to prove something to someone, then status is an important factor in weighing job offers. But if you're working to provide for yourself and your family, as I believe you should be, status on its own is meaningless. Status alone won't put food on the table or pay for your daughter's college tuition. Status will make a difference only with people shallow enough to believe you are what you do and your value as a human being is primarily determined by your work. Another important point to consider is that high-status jobs often require larger-than-average time commitments. High-status people often think of themselves as being "too important" to go home at five, or to take two weeks' vacation. They have to stay late and take working vacations. High-status people don't have the time to go to their son's Little League game or their daughter's dance recital. Even if they don't think of themselves that way, many others do, and the expectation becomes a reality.

*Title.* Don't let meaningless labels influence your choice of jobs. Some companies continue to try to entice people into taking less money in exchange for a more exalted-sounding title. The son of a client of mine was offered a job as "editor in chief" of a small-town weekly newspaper. Of course, the job included everything from writing all the stories to delivering the paper door to door. While that's an extreme example, it's indicative of the kind of title inflation that's taken place in the past few years. There are no more secretaries . . . they're all administrative assistants. There are no more sales clerks . . . they're all customer service representatives. Even while all this title inflation is taking place there are other cutting-edge companies that are coming up with either stylistic titles—"manger of creative destruction" is one of my favorites—or removing titles altogether, pursing some kind of classless vision of a workplace filled with "comrades." Because the practical value of titles in determining exactly what you do has diminished, even the most traditional recruiter ignores them in reviewing a résumé. Job descriptions are what matter today, not titles. That's why I had you draft your own job description back in chapter 2. The titles that matter most today are husband, wife, life partner, father, mother, and friend.

## Factors That May or May Not Be Important

There are a handful of job-offer characteristics that may or may not be important to consider, depending on their specifics and/or your current life circumstances.

*Disability insurance.* I'm a big believer in the importance of disability insurance. That's because when I was forty-eight years old I contracted tuberculosis and lost my job as a vice president at a major bank. Until I recovered and launched a new career as an attorney and life coach, I relied on my disability-insurance benefits to help keep food on my family's table and a roof over our heads.[11] While Social Security does indeed have a disability-insurance element, it is very difficult to qualify for benefits, and the payouts are quite low. If you don't have a disability-insurance policy of your own, receiving one as a benefit is definitely an important factor in weighing a job offer. It's also an important factor if you would for some reason have a hard time obtaining an affordable disability policy on your own. Since employers purchase insurance coverages as group plans, one individual employee's health shouldn't have an impact on coverage or cost. If you already have disability coverage of your own, this isn't an important factor in judging a job offer.

*Health insurance.* You don't need me to explain how important

---

11. My illness and subsequent recovery had, as you might imagine, a profound effect on my attitudes toward life and work. Those are outlined and explored in my book *Second Acts*.

health insurance is today. If you don't have it from another source, it's a definite plus in any job compensation package. But if you are already, or can be, covered by someone else's health plan, it need not be a factor in choosing one job offer over another. Don't get me wrong. Having secondary coverage isn't worthless. It might pick up some of the out-of-pocket costs not covered by the primary coverage. So if all else is equal between two offers, you might as well take the one that provides health insurance.

*Life insurance.* While I'm a big proponent of disability insurance, I'm not a big fan of life insurance. I think people usually carry far too much life coverage and it's usually of the wrong kind. I tell my clients they should have only as much life insurance as necessary for their family to maintain their lifestyle for three years—that's enough time to make adjustments—and to take care of any outstanding obligations— the remaining contributions to a child's college savings plan, for example. And I think the only type of insurance that's worth buying is pure term that has the same premium for either a five- or a fifteen-year period. I don't believe insurance is ever really a good investment vehicle.[12] So why don't I list life insurance as an unimportant factor? One reason only. If you cannot obtain affordable life insurance on your own, say because of a medical condition, you will probably be able to get it through an employer's group plan. Therefore, if this is the only way you can get life insurance coverage, it's an important factor to consider.

*Retirement plan.* I'm lumping together all employer-sponsored investment plans in this category. These are important factors only if the employer funds the plan, in whole or in part. If there's no employer financial contribution involved, and you'll be funding the plan entirely on

12. The exception to my term-only rule is when a senior citizen needs a policy to cover burial expenses. Term policies actually cost more than whole-life policies when the insured is over a certain age.

your own, it really doesn't matter which company offers what plan. You can always save more money on your own to compensate. But if you're considering two jobs, one that offers a 401(k) plan in which the employer matches employee contributions dollar for dollar, and one that doesn't offer this type of matching program, it would be an important factor to consider. After all, those contributions are, or at least will be, a definite boost to your income. Alternatively, if one potential employer offers a defined-benefit pension plan—the amount of your payout is guaranteed—and the other offers a defined-contribution pension plan—the amount of its deposit is the only thing that's certain—the former may be a real advantage, worth weighing heavily when making your choice.

*Tuition reimbursement.* Tuition reimbursement is an important factor only if your own long-term plans mesh with the restrictions and limitations placed on the reimbursement plan. For instance, some firms will only reimburse tuition for certain courses of study that, in theory, will have a direct short-term impact on your job performance. That would be a positive factor only if those specific courses of study fit into your long-term plan. Let's say you're working for an engineering firm that will reimburse tuition for courses leading to a master's in engineering. Your long-term plan involves moving into a management role rather than staying with engineering. In that case the reimbursement offer really isn't an important factor to consider in weighing the offer. Another way to look at it is, if you'd be paying for the education on your own anyway, this is an important factor; otherwise, it's not.

## Factors That Are Important Today

So what are the important factors when weighing job offers today? I believe there are five issues on which you need to focus. This time I'll address them in order of importance.

*Income.* Nearly everyone says he wants to make more money. Then why is it so few of us make it a priority in our work life? I think for both psychological and cultural reasons we believe money is crass, venal, and dirty. Yet money in and of itself can do nothing. Its value is entirely extrinsic. Money is simply a means of exchange, a tool. And a tool is neither good nor evil. It can be powerful, however. Money may not be able to buy happiness, but it can buy things that make you happy, and its absence can make you unhappy. Money may not be able to buy you health—since you can't purchase new genes—but it can sure buy you preventive care and better medical treatment if you do get ill. Money can't buy you the spiritual love of another human being. But it can buy you physical love—prostitution was probably one of the first uses for money—and it can buy you a form of spiritual love, albeit from pets rather than from human beings.

There's nothing wrong with making money the priority in choosing which job offer you accept. As I've said earlier, work is the only aspect of life that has the potential to provide you with money. You can get spiritual, psychological, and emotional fulfillment from your personal life. In fact, you're more likely to get that kind of fulfillment from your personal life than from your work life. If you want more money, make it the priority in your work life. That's really the unspoken secret in the American workplace. The way to make more money is to make it your priority. Those who earn a great deal of money do so because they spend a lot of time and energy in the effort to make money. They stress the importance of money in all their work and business actions. They make it their number one priority. So should you. In fact, you should make every effort possible to trade any of the compensation benefits I've listed as unimportant factors for additional money. (See the box on page 169: Trading Benefits for Dollars or Time Off.)

As I've said before: do it for the money and the love will follow. To the extent that you maximize the amount of money you earn through

## TRADING BENEFITS FOR DOLLARS OR TIME OFF

Just because a particular benefit isn't important enough to you to be part of your weighing a job offer doesn't mean it's something you should forget about. Many of these benefits impact a potential employer's bottom line. By forgoing, say, health insurance, you can save your potential employer a great deal of money. By pointing this out during your salary negotiations you may be able to get additional income or paid time off. The key is to frame this, not as asking for more, but as asking for a credit for something you're giving up. It will probably be easier to ask for additional paid time off—say another week's vacation—than additional dollars.

work, you maximize your chances to satisfy your other needs outside of work. More money from work provides you with the tools to do more with the rest of your life. Money from work provides you with the means to travel, to help the poor, to provide for your children, to paint watercolors of the Southwest, to buy books, to go to museums and films and concerts, to take classes, to do whatever it is you love, whatever makes you happiest.

Of course, you also need the time to do all those things you love, and that's why I believe you also need to give priority to the next three factors.

*Proximity.* I'm always amazed how little people take their proximity to the workplace into account when choosing one job over another. Some people spend more time going to and from work during the course of a week than they spend interacting one-on-one with their children, and that's a shame. Let's take the stereotypical couple with children who have moved from an urban environment to a suburban one in order to provide a better quality of life for their children. Say it takes, door to door, ninety minutes for the husband to get from home to his workplace, and sixty minutes, door to door, for the wife to get from home to her workplace. That's three hours a day and fifteen hours a week for the husband, spent traveling to and from work. For the wife it's two hours a day and ten hours a week. Added together that's more than a day that this hypothetical couple spends traveling to and from work. That's twenty-five hours spent neither earning money nor spending time on the things that fulfill you personally—other than possibly reading if the trip is on mass transit, or listening to music if it's in a personal car. If they each took a job that was just thirty minutes closer, they could conceivably have breakfast with their kids in the morning, or get home early enough to play before dinner. And of course this applies to things other than spending time with the family. The added time could be spent going to a museum after work, or going to a movie during the week, since they wouldn't have to wake up as early.

Besides the lifestyle benefit of being closer to work, there's also a financial benefit. How can you calculate the financial value of less time spent commuting? Well, one way is to take your weekly salary and divide that by the total of the hours you spend traveling to and from work and the hours you actually spend at work. Say you spend two hours a day commuting and you work eight hours a day. That's a total of ten hours a day and fifty hours a week. Let's also say, for simplicity's sake, you gross $1,000 a week. That means, commuting included, you're earning $20 per hour. Say you are offered a job that pays the same $1,000 a week, but that is thirty minutes closer to your home. That's one hour a day and five hours a week you save in travel. Instead of dividing the $1,000 by fifty hours, divide it by forty-five hours. Your hourly earnings, calculated in this manner, would increase to $22.22 per hour. That's the equivalent of an extra $111 a week, and $5,772 a year. Add the potential lifestyle advantages to the additional equivalent of $5,772 a year, and the nearer job is the better choice.

*Paid time off.* The third important factor to consider when weighing jobs today is how much paid time off you get at each job. The more paid time off you get, the more time you have to spend on your personal life, doing the things that are more likely to give you psychological, emotional, and spiritual fulfillment, without paying a financial price for that fulfillment. In effect, you get to have your cake and eat it too; you get to spend time on your personal life while being paid by your employer. While two weeks' paid vacation has become the standard in the American workplace, there are many organizations that offer more days, based on years of service, and that also allow you to accumulate unused paid sick and personal days. I'd suggest that if you can't trade any of the unimportant factors for money, you try to trade them for additional paid time off. I'd rather see you get another week's vacation than a better title and a company car.

*Unpaid time off.* While it's not as valuable as paid time off, unpaid time off is also an important factor to weigh when comparing jobs. Temporary leaves to handle family matters can be invaluable in a crisis. The psychological comfort you receive from knowing your job will be waiting for you when you return from welcoming a newborn into your home, easing an aging parent into a new living situation, or attending to a death in the family is incalculable. Sabbaticals, while offered by only a handful of employers, are incredible opportunities to spend an extended period of time doing something that brings fulfillment. Being able to spend six months traveling through Europe or helping Habitat for Humanity build low-income housing in West Virginia, and being able to come back to your job after such an experience, is a rare opportunity and it should be treasured.

*Opportunity for learning.* A much more common opportunity, which I don't think is treasured enough, is the chance to expand your skills and knowledge on the job. An opportunity for learning is an opportunity to increase your future job-fishing prospects. Whether it's studying and absorbing the dynamics of a new industry, or picking up a new technical skill, learning opportunities will turn you into a more desirable employee in the future. This is one of the few things your current employer will ever do to help you land your next job. This can sometimes be such an important factor that I've actually encouraged a handful of clients over the years to take a lesser-paying job just for the chance to pick up a new skill. The idea is that by taking one step back financially they will set themselves up to take a larger step ahead with their next job by adding a skill to their repertoire that exponentially increases their value. An example that comes quickly to mind is Rachel Mizrahi, a client who worked as managing editor of a women's magazine. She took a job with a start-up that was founding a woman-oriented health Web site in the early 1990s even though it meant a small cut in her pay. After only a year working at the Web site she was offered a job heading up the publications department of a medical school, based at least in part on her having both magazine and Web site experience. That job paid $20,000 more than she was previously earning, an income jump she wouldn't have achieved as quickly without having first taken that step back in exchange for an opportunity to learn.

## Prioritizing the Factors in Two Job Offers

Turn back to the chart you created comparing your competing job offers. Get yourself a Hi-Liter or a red pen. Highlight the lines in the chart that represent the factors which are truly important to you. In addition to the five I believe are important to everyone—income, proximity, paid time off, unpaid time off, and opportunity for learning—include any of the five neutral factors—disability insurance, health insurance, life insurance, retirement plan, tuition reimbursement—that are important in this instance.

Now compare the two offers, focusing on only these factors. Is one offer clearly better than the other? I'll bet that by prioritizing in this fashion you're able to take a debatable choice and make it clearer. However, if you're still unable to clearly chose one over the other, my advice would be to choose the one that pays a higher income. Never forget that when it comes to work, it's the money that matters most.

## Debbie O'Leary Prioritizes the Factors in Her Two Job Offers

Debbie went back to her chart and highlighted the five important factors. On the income line, the satellite job had the advantage. On the proximity line, the radio job came out on top. While the radio job also had the advantage of offering more unpaid time off, the satellite job provided more paid time off. The satellite job also offered opportunities for learning. Since neither job offered disability or life insurance, or tuition reimbursement, those factors weren't important. Debbie already had health insurance coverage through her husband, so that wasn't an important factor either. However, the satellite radio job had a retirement plan that included an employer financial contribution, effectively adding to her income and making it an important factor to consider. Weighing the factors that really are important today, Debbie surprised herself (and her husband) by opting for the satellite radio job . . . the offer she had almost reflexively turned down. I gave her a round of applause, both in congratulations and as a small substitute for the public fanfare she'd be missing. But then I told her she still had more work to do: she had to figure out when she'd be leaving the job she'd just started.

# CHAPTER 8

# Hello, I Must Be Going

*Hello, I must be going.*
*I came to say,*
*I cannot stay,*
*I must be going.*

—Groucho Marx in *Animal Crackers*

AGGIE WICKFIELD HAD never felt so empowered when leaving a job. After eighteen months as administrative assistant to the comptroller of an outdoor-clothing manufacturing firm, Aggie was leaving, of her own volition, to take a job as personal assistant to the president of a labor union. Every other time she had left a job it had been because she either hated the job or was laid off. But she didn't hate her job with the clothing manufacturer. In fact, she liked it. It paid well and provided her with the chance to learn some new skills. And far from laying her off, her boss was sad to see her go, fearful of not being able to replace her. Aggie was leaving because she had found something even better; a job that provided more of the benefits of her current job, as well as some things it lacked. The job with the labor union paid better, provided chances to learn even more new skills, gave more paid holidays, and was located closer to her home. For the first time in her working life Aggie felt as if she were moving toward something, rather than away from something. She realized she was moving toward being happier.

You can choose the time you leave a job, rather than waiting for the ax to fall.

You can repeatedly move from good jobs to better jobs, instead of moving from one bad job to another.

You can guarantee you get more of what you want from work simply by choosing to shift jobs in order to improve your situation.

You can turn your work life from a reactive process in which you feel pushed around by chance and uncaring bosses, to a proactive course in which you are in charge, moving when and where you want.

To achieve this you need to adopt the seventh and final element in my work philosophy, one I call "Hello, I must be going." What this means is that, having gone job fishing and landed a number of job offers, and having chosen the best one, you enter that job with the clear sense of why and how you'll leave it. You accept that every job is temporary, and plan accordingly.

## We Are All Hired to Be Fired

In professional sports leagues, only one team wins a championship. That means every other team in the league ends up a loser, regardless of how entertaining its games were, or how much its record improved over previous years. Because of this, coaches or managers are constantly being fired. After all, unless they win the championship they've failed at their job. The adage is that a coach or manager is hired to be fired.

What's true of professional sports is true of all work today. We are all hired to be fired. A company brings in a group of people to, let's say, create an e-commerce operation for the company. If it generates immediate profits or boosts the stock price, they keep their jobs and keep the operation going. If after, perhaps, two years, the e-commerce operation isn't working, or hasn't helped push up the stock price, the whole project is shelved and everyone is fired. This goes not just for new ventures, but for long-standing elements of an organization. Outsource the bookkeeping department. Replace the sales staff with independent reps. Computerize customer service and fire the whole team.

People used to be viewed as assets of a business, a part of the long-term wealth and value of the organization. Today, people are seen as expenses, to be added or cut depending on what's needed to impact the short-term revenues, or worse, stock price, of the company.

You can blame this on the acceleration of the business cycle, the globalization of commerce, or advances in information technology. You can blame it on the current presidential administration, Congress, or Wall Street. You can even blame the tides or the signs of the zodiac. On the practical level, where and who we work for a living all exist, it doesn't matter who's to blame. What matters is the facts on the ground . . . and how you react to them. This what I tried to explain to Bill Kaplan when he first came to see me.

As I noted back in chapter 1, Bill is a recent college graduate who led a pretty unsettled and nomadic life up until graduation. The son of a longtime client of mine, Bill is a charming and very creative young man. At times it seemed his creativity was more of a curse than a blessing, since he could never quite figure out how to harness it.

After high school he went to a small private college in upstate New York with the intent of being a fine-arts major. But while there he was bitten by the acting bug. Convinced that was where his future lay, he transferred from the arts school to a state university, where he became a theater arts major. After a year studying theater he decided the only way to really become an actor was to act, and so, despite his parents' pleas, he dropped out of college, moved to New York City, took jobs waiting on tables, and tried to line up acting work. After two years of struggle he went back to school at a city college, this time to pursue his love of writing and reading. He became an English major and finally graduated.

Having become fascinated by the bookstore business, Bill was thrilled to line up a job as an assistant manager at one of the large chain bookstores. He came to see me for a life-planning session, at the suggestion of his parents. After hearing him wax enthusiastic about his new job I explained that everyone, including him, had actually been hired to be fired, and suggested he start laying the groundwork to leave.

## Leave Before You're Pushed Out

I don't think anyone who's been in the job market for the past few years, or who has read the newspapers or watched the news recently, can disagree that today we're all hired to be fired. No one's job is secure for the long term, whether you're the last hired or a lifelong employee, a star performer or a slacker, making minimum wage or six figures. As a result, I think it's essential that you leave before you're pushed out.

As I've touched on earlier in this book, if you wait until you're terminated to look for work, you'll find yourself a seller in a buyer's market. If your employer is cutting staff, you'll be competing with your former coworkers for any job openings elsewhere. If your old company is cutting back, odds are that other firms in the same industry are doing the same, making the number of job seekers out there even larger and the number of potential employers lower. And if multiple companies in your industry are cutting back, that could have a ripple effect on support industries and businesses, adding to the number of unemployed and subtracting from the number of possible openings. In addition, an industry-wide cutback could be indicative of a larger economic trend, meaning many other industries are ailing too. That means still more job seekers and still fewer potential employers.

Greg Horn loved his job as a pilot with a small commuter airline in New England. He enjoyed flying the company's small turboprops and being able to spend almost every night at home with his wife and newborn son. That's why, when he began sensing things weren't going well with his employer, he hesitated to look for another job. By early 2002, when he was laid off, all the other small commuter airlines in New England were cutting staff as well because of the industry slowdown. It wasn't until the middle of 2003 that he was able to find another flying job.

On the other hand, if you leave on your own you'll be a seller in a seller's market. You won't be competing with others from your company who were fired. There won't be a slew of terminations from other companies in your industry. In fact, they may be interested in stealing away people from a competitor when times are good. If your industry is doing well, the support industries will be fine too. And unless your industry runs counter to the business cycle, other industries will probably be doing well too.

John Carpinose had been in the private security industry for more than a decade. After graduating college with a degree in criminal justice he had joined one of the country's larger com-

## TIPS FOR GETTING RAISES

There are only four arguments you can make to get more money from your boss:

1. Your income hasn't kept pace with the cost of living because of inflation.

2. You're making an exceptional contribution to the company's bottom line.

3. You've taken on new tasks and responsibilities, so your job has changed.

4. You're not being paid the market rate for your services.

There's no acceptable reason for an employer to turn down a cost-of-living increase. However, it's not actually a raise, since all you're doing is keeping pace with inflation.

If your contribution is a onetime occurrence, you're liable to receive a bonus rather than a raise. Still, that's better than nothing.

Having taken on new responsibilities, you're due added compensation, but only if the company values your increased contributions.

Showing that you're not being paid market value puts the company on the spot. To keep you they'll have to give you a raise. Whatever they do, there will be a positive outcome. If they value you as an employee they'll come across with more money. If they don't give you a raise it means they don't value you, they don't have the money, or both. Whatever the reason, this means you should take another job as soon as possible.

mercial security companies. A skilled manager who was willing to travel because he was single, John became one of the company's "firefighters," rapidly responding to divisions or regions that had problems. The growing pains in the business after Sep-

tember 11 had spawned more than the usual number of crises.
Yet John still made time for his job fishing. It yielded four offers
from other security-related companies in the span of six
months. John was able to get a 50 percent increase in salary by
jumping to a competitor in the midst of the business boom.

## Leave Something on the Table

Over the past couple of years some of my more enterprising clients
have come to me for help in trying to perfectly time leaving their job.
They accept that they were hired to be fired and need to leave before
they're pushed out, but don't want to miss out in the process. They
want to keep their job as long as they're still likely to get raises and
bonuses, but leave just as their potential for increasing their income
has peaked. (See the box on page 179: Tips for Getting Raises.) These
people are trying to do in the job market what others attempt in the
stock market or in financial negotiations.

Stock market timers try to hold on to a stock as long as it continues
to increase in value, only selling it at its top price, just before it starts
going down, so they get every single penny from it they possibly can.
Greedy negotiators want to hold out until they either get every last
dollar the other party was willing to spend, or force every last conces-
sion possible. They want to sell for the highest price possible and buy
for the lowest price possible.

I tell my clients they should feel free to time their job status this
way . . . just as soon as they've shown me they can do the same with
the stock market or in negotiations. I don't mean to be flippant, but no
one has ever figured out how to consistently time the stock market in
this way. People always sell before a stock reaches its top price—and
kick themselves for missing out on a few dollars more—or sell once it

has started going down in price—and kick themselves for not selling sooner and missing out on a few dollars more. And no one has ever figured out how to always get every single dollar out of a negotiation. My advice to those trying to time the job market is the same as those trying to time the stock market or max out their negotiations: don't.

Most people make the mistake of thinking there are discrete, readily apparent moments in the rise and fall of something they're watching closely, whether it's a stock price, financial concessions, or earnings potential from a job. High and low points can be seen only in hindsight. It's only after something has started going down, after it has passed its tipping point, that you can see where and when it reached its peak or hit its bottom. The only way to be able to discern the high point or low point is to wait until it has passed. That's why, whether it comes to the stock market, negotiating, or deciding when to leave a job, I advocate "leaving something on the table."

Success in these situations isn't getting every last penny; it's getting a result with which you're happy. When it comes to the stock market, that means selling or buying at a price which works, not just at the highest or lowest price. When it comes to negotiating, that means reaching an agreement with which both parties are comfortable, not just when one side has gotten everything possible out of the other. And when it comes to leaving your job, that means, if possible, leaving while you're still valued, while you're still getting raises. In all these instances, greed will get the better of you if you let it. Instead, be willing to settle for less than everything. Believe me, if you leave a job at a time when you might have been able to get another raise, you'll make up for it in your next job.

Elizabeth Stoerdeur felt a bit guilty accepting the employee of the year award from the specialty cable network where she worked, because she knew she was going to be leaving in less than a month. Elizabeth had just been promoted and given a raise for being the driving force behind the network's surprise hit of the fall season. At the network's annual Christmas party two executive producers had separately pulled her aside to pass on the rumor that she was in line for the next executive producer opening. She bit her lip and didn't tell either that, knowing how fleeting success in the media business could be, she had already accepted an executive producer job at another cable network.

## Covert Versus Overt Approaches

You and I and everyone else in the world who's been conscious during the past few years realizes there's no job security anymore, and that employees are hired to be fired. But that doesn't mean bosses are ready to admit it—at least not to all their employees.

If you're a lower- or midlevel worker, bosses will show you no loyalty and will fire you at the drop of a share price, but they don't want to see that you're preparing for that to happen and, heaven forbid, could beat them to the punch. Bosses are very uncomfortable with assertive and empowered workers. Despite all evidence to the contrary, they will preach to you about loyalty and security and opportunities for growth and advancement in the company. They're afraid that if they admit the truth you'll be apt to leave as soon as you get a better offer somewhere else. They're right. Still, for you to get the most you can out of this job for the limited amount of time you'll be there, you need to play dumb. Do everything you can to meet your boss's needs, as I explained earlier, and keep your plans for leaving undercover.

If you're an upper-level executive, however, you're considered part of the club. They think you're a professional, a peer, rather than a

## GETTING IT IN WRITING

Employment contracts are all custom documents. All that's required is that they include compensation figures and an agreed-upon term of employment. Other than that, anything can be included. And my suggestion is that if you're getting some details in writing, you may as well get all the details in writing. Include information on benefits, retirement plan contributions, bonuses, raises, vacations, sick days, personal leave, severance pay, duties, even your place in the hierarchy.

I know it's not easy to get employers to sign employment contracts. My clients have had success getting them using three different techniques. Some have successfully transformed raise negotiations into employment-contract negotiations. Others have used job offers from competitors as leverage to get a contract with their existing employer. But perhaps the most effective strategy is to ask for an employment contract and then negotiate a compromise by getting a termination agreement.

This works by playing to the ego of your boss. The conversation usually goes something like this. You ask for a contract and your boss says the company doesn't issue employment contracts. Rather than giving up you say your primary concern is being terminated without cause. Your boss rises to the challenge and says the company "never terminates anyone without cause." You quickly agree, saying you have total confidence in him and the current management, but what if the company is sold? Since you both *know* that your boss and the current management would never terminate without cause, drawing up a simple termination agreement would just be an emotional security blanket for you. Seven times out of ten this works.

lowly worker or subordinate manager. Employers will be less uncomfortable with one of their own club being empowered. Since they'll see you as being on their level, they won't pretend there's any loyalty in the workplace. Their willingness to acknowledge the inevitability of your leaving opens up the potential for overt action on your part. The best actions you can take are to negotiate either an employment contract or a termination agreement that defines exactly what you're entitled to when you're fired. (See the box on page 183: Getting It in Writing.)

> Liam Nolan is respected in the antique business as one of the leading appraisers of vintage firearms. When the large auction house for which he worked became embroiled in controversy, Liam stepped up his job fishing and landed an offer at another major auction house. But as part of his deal, Liam asked for an employment contract. The auction house, while desperate to steal Liam from a competitor, had a policy against employment contracts. The head of human resources there was willing to sign a termination agreement, however. I helped Liam behind the scenes, but he and the human resources director were able to hammer out a fair agreement over a couple of collegial lunches. The agreement spelled out that Liam was entitled to a year's severance plus continued medical benefits at the company's expense for up to two years, or until he landed another job.

## What Brought You to This Job Will Lead to Your Next Job

Whether or not you're part of the executive club, you need to come up with your own checklist for when you'll be leaving your new job. Note that I used the word "checklist" rather than "timeline" or "schedule." You should be basing your job shifts not on how long you've been in a particular position, but on whether or not you can obtain improvements in the factors you use in judging job offers.

I tell my clients that one of the most important things they need to do in their first week on a new job is prepare a job factor checklist. Since you probably received so many job offers from all your successful personal networking, I assume you haven't any blank charts left over from chapter 7. That means the first thing you need to do is turn back to page 152 and make another copy of that blank chart. Don't do this at the office copy machine, however. While I think you should be ready to leave from day one, you want to do it on your own terms. Walking around the office with a copy of a book titled *Fire Your Boss* may lead to trouble, especially in your first week. I'd suggest you take a few minutes out of one evening that first week to go through this exercise.

Start by crossing off the words Offer #1 on top of the second column and instead write Current Job in that space. Now, go down the list of twenty factors, filling in information on what your current job provides in each area. If you're not sure of the information, leave it blank and consult the employee handbook or human resources department the next time you're in the office. Since you've only been there a week, questions about these kinds of details will be seen as the sort of standard fact finding every new employee engages in, rather than a sign of impending departure.

Use a pencil when you're filling in the chart this time, however. That's because every time you get a raise, a promotion, or a transfer, and any time the circumstances of the job somehow change, you will need to update this chart. Obviously this isn't something you're going to hang on the wall behind your desk. Keep it at home in the same place you keep all your important papers and documents.

Before you file the paper away, take a few moments to look it over. Starting tomorrow you'll be back job fishing again. Your hoped-for catch is an offer of a position that provides more, in any or all of the twenty factors, than you're currently receiving. It's essential that you have a clear picture of your intended catch, your next job, in mind within two weeks of starting a new job. That doesn't mean you're going to jump at the first better offer that comes along, of course.

## Bill Kaplan Fills Out a Job Factor Chart

In order to have a baseline against which to compare job offers, Bill Kaplan needed to fill out a job factor chart for his current job as assistant manager of the bookstore.

On the amenities line, Bill noted that the bookstore offered a very large employee discount on merchandise purchased.

There was no auto provided, so Bill left the next line blank.

Since this was Bill's first nonwaiter job it presented quite a few challenges, primarily learning how to manage employees and the dynamics of the bookstore business. Bill wrote those items down on his chart.

The culture of the organization was a mixed bag for Bill. It was very supportive of employees but tended to be a bit controlling. Bill joked that it was a nonthreatening cult, and actually used that phrase on his chart.

The company didn't provide any disability insurance, so that line was left blank.

The environment in which Bill worked was quite pleasant, and he wrote that on his chart. The store itself was comfortable and was located in a large regional mall that, while sterile, offered many conveniences.

The company provided employees with a weekly stipend that could be used at the coffee shop in the store, so Bill noted that on the expense allowance line.

The company provided health insurance through an HMO that, while severely restricting Bill's choice of doctors, paid almost all his medical costs. Bill wrote "restrictive but comprehensive" on the health insurance line of the chart.

Bill's salary as an assistant manager was $35,000 a year. He noted that on the income line of his chart.

The company offered no life insurance, so that line was left blank.

The organization prided itself on promoting from within; however, those promotions invariably required a move to another store. Bill wrote "many if willing to relocate" on the opportunity for advancement line of his chart.

Working in the bookstore offered Bill some opportunity for learning since he could learn the music side of the business as well as the buying process. He simply wrote "yes" on that line of the chart.

Bill noted that he received one week's paid vacation and three paid personal days in his first year of employment.

The bookstore was a thirty-minute drive each way from Bill's apartment, so he wrote "one-hour round-trip" on the proximity line of his chart.

The company offered a retirement savings plan but didn't match contributions until an employee had spent three years at the company. Bill made note of that limitation on his chart.

As the number two national chain, Bill noted, the company had moderate relative stability. That's because it wasn't as stable as the number one chain, but it was far more stable than an independent store or a regional chain.

Bill didn't think managing a bookstore had any real status, so he wrote "none" on that line of his chart.

He wrote "assistant manager" on the title line of his chart, adding that there appeared to be so few titles in the business that the whole issue was "unimportant."

Since the company didn't provide any tuition reimbursement, Bill left that line on the chart blank.

On the final line, Bill noted that the company offered one week of unpaid parental leave and three unpaid personal days a year.

Bill hung the completed chart on his refrigerator door with a couple of magnets. He found that looking at it every morning when he made his breakfast provided him with the impetus to keep on fishing for other offers. After six months, Bill received an automatic salary bonus to $37,000, so he updated that line of the chart. (See the box on page 189: Bill Kaplan's Job Factor Chart.)

## Timing Your Next Move

When is it time to actually leave your job and take one of the better offers you've been soliciting through your job fishing and comparing to your job factor chart? Well, it depends.

As I wrote back in chapter 7, I think you can divide the twenty common job factors into three categories: unimportant, potentially important, and definitely important. The unimportant factors are amenities, auto, challenging, culture, environment, expense allowance, opportunity for advancement, stability, status, and title. The factors that may or may not be important, depending on the specifics and your particular circumstances, are disability insurance, health insurance, life insurance, retirement plan, and tuition reimbursement. The factors that are definitely of the most importance to everyone are income, opportunity for learning, paid time off, proximity, and unpaid time off.

## BILL KAPLAN'S JOB FACTOR CHART

| FACTOR | CURRENT JOB | NEXT JOB? |
|---|---|---|
| Amenities | employee discount | |
| Auto | | |
| Challenging | managing people bookstore business | |
| Culture | nonthreatening cult | |
| Disability insurance | | |
| Environment | pleasant, convenient but sterile | |
| Expense allowance | weekly stipend for coffee shop | |
| Health insurance | restrictive but comprehensive | |
| Income | ~~$35,000~~ $37,000 | |
| Life insurance | | |
| Opportunity for advancement | many, if willing to relocate | |
| Opportunity for learning | yes | |
| Paid time off | 1 week plus 3 days | |
| Proximity | one-hour round-trip | |
| Retirement plan | will contribute after 3 years | |
| Stability | moderate relative stability | |
| Status | none | |
| Title | assistant manager— unimportant | |
| Tuition reimbursement | | |
| Unpaid time off | 1 week parental plus 3 personal days | |

While everyone's situation is different, I can offer you some general guidelines I've come up with to help my clients.

If you've been at your current job for less than one year, I'd suggest you consider only those offers that provide an improvement in at least two important factors. In other words, give serious thought to offers of jobs that, let's say, offer more money *and* are located closer to your home. Job hopping—moving rapidly from job to job—isn't frowned on today as it was in the past. And shifting jobs in less than a year won't trouble the company hiring you away—they'll see it as a coup. But it might give second thoughts to subsequent companies. They will see that you've shifted jobs in less than a year, and that you're still continuing to look for another job. While the first company will think they've "stolen away" someone who's ambitious, subsequent companies will worry you're erratic and unpredictable. Sparking such concerns is worthwhile only if you're making a considerable improvement in your work life.

> When Lisa Frankfort graduated from massage school she immediately took a job with an exclusive health club in Manhattan. She grabbed the job because, as a single mother in New York City, she needed to bring in an income as soon as possible. Within eight months of taking that job she received a job offer from a physical therapy practice located in Queens. Not only was that job within walking distance of her apartment and her son's school, but it paid $10,000 more than her job with the health club. Despite being in her first job for only eight months, she leaped at the new offer.

If you've been at your job for between one and two years, my advice would be to consider seriously any offer that provides an improvement in one of the important factors. You're now past the point where changing jobs might have an impact on your image. You're also past the point where you've either received or been denied a salary increase. That could mean you've maxed out your earnings with this company. Many companies will give a decent raise to a new employee after a year as a way to cement the relationship. Quite often the raise simply brings the person up to the maximum amount the company would have paid to fill the job in the first place. In any case, getting another sizable increase the second year becomes more problematic. I call it the sophomore jinx. You're no longer the potential savior or the rising star. You're just one more expense line. That's why you should be ready to jump for another position that gives you any increase in an important factor.

In his eighteen months with the symphony of a midsize New England city, Jerry Pryor had rejuvenated the percussion section. The first new hire in that section for more than a decade, Jerry revitalized a moribund element of the orchestra. That was reflected in his first raise after only ten months. Since then, however, he had become a fixture in an organization that was unused to much changeover. He could almost feel himself receding into the background. But before he disappeared into the shadows Jerry decided to accept an offer to join the orchestra of a nationally known opera company in a small Mid-Atlantic city. The job was identical to his current position, except it paid about 10 percent more than he was earning with the symphony.

If you've been at your job for more than two years, I'd suggest you seriously consider any offer that provides an improvement in any of the factors, important or not. In today's job market, two years is a lifetime. You're on your way to becoming an icon of the company . . . and that's the last thing you want nowadays. I know it sounds radical, but I'd encourage you at this point to make a move to any job that represents a positive step. You must keep moving to stay alive in today's job market. I'd prefer you make an external move, since it will lead to more money. But if you must, investigate internal transfers as well. If you don't move soon you will find yourself sinking in quicksand.

> Sam Betts loved working with wood. A fine-arts major in college, Sam first tried making it as a sculptor in New York. But after only a few months starving he found his way to a job at a custom cabinet shop on the Upper West Side of Manhattan. He knew right away he'd found his niche. Apprenticing with the owner, Sam became a skilled cabinetmaker, specializing in custom library bookcases. After two years Sam had become recognized in the business as the best in New York at what he did. The owner no longer looked over Sam's shoulder when he worked. In his third year in the business, people had begun requesting Sam's work, but using the name of the cabinet shop. Sam realized he was becoming too closely identified with the business. When he received an offer to work as a cabinetmaker for a custom builder in suburban Westchester County, Sam jumped at the job, even though the only added benefit was a bit more prestige.

## Jumping Ship in Troubled Waters

Tenure isn't the only consideration for when you should take another job. The relative stability or instability of your current employer needs to considered as well. You know all jobs are temporary today . . . but some are more temporary than others. The traditional response to an unstable situation has been to try to ride it out. I think that's a mistake. In fact, I think it's a kind of workplace denial.

Let's say you're one of five department managers in the regional office of a large company. You get word that the general manager of your regional office is being fired, and replaced with someone who managed one of the smaller regional offices for the company. While your initial reflex may be concern, the denial muscle soon starts twitching. You think maybe this new person coming in won't be bad. He'll have an open mind and will want to keep people, like you, who know what they're doing and will help him meet his needs. Then you start thinking about all the faults of the general manager who's being replaced. Soon you start thinking the new person may even be a savior, correcting all past faults, leading the department on to greater glory.

Wrong. Your first instinct was the right one. This is trouble, and you should get out while the getting is good.

This new person coming in has sold the company a bill of goods about how he is going to "clean up" your office, "light a fire under" the underperforming staff, "upgrade" the department. You can pick any of a hundred different clichés. Suffice it to say he was brought in to make changes, not keep things the same. If the company wanted things to stay the same they wouldn't have fired the previous general manager. What's the easiest way for the new boss to make changes quickly? What's the best way for him to show the people who promoted him that he's on the ball? Deep down you know the answer. He's going to fire people. Most of the assistant managers will soon be gone. One may survive long enough for the new team to pick his or her brains clean. You might think you can survive by assiduously working to fill the needs of this new boss. That's not impossible. But odds are he will be bringing his own people along with him. And the first person he'll bring is the subordinate at his old office who was doing the best job helping him meet his needs there.

Your boss being fired is just one scenario that should lead you to quickly take another job. There are others.

If your company is purchased by another firm, get another job quick. The new firm will have its own "culture," which those of you who worked for the old firm will never be able to adopt fully. This will always be a company divided into "us" and "them." And as an employee of the purchased company you're one of "them." Believe me, soon all of "them" will be gone.

If your company's owners sell out to new owners, get another job quick. The new owners will, much like the new general manager I described in the earlier example, want to make changes simply to show who's in charge and that times have changed.

If your company merges with another company, get another job quick. You'll start hearing words like "synergy" and phrases like "duplication of effort." The new merged company will first fire half its employees and then, over time, will replace the remaining half with entirely new people, untainted by either of the previous incarnations.

If your company shows any signs of financial difficulty, get another job quick. You may hear talk of shared sacrifices, of belt-tightening, of fresh infusions of capital, or of restructuring. You may even read stories about reorganization to avoid bankruptcy, or hear rumors of possible mergers and buyouts. Some of this talk may actually be true. But it doesn't matter. Financial trouble for the company spells financial trouble for you. And remember, you're doing this for the money.

Whenever you're facing a very unstable work situation, act as if you've been on the job for more than two years and grab the best offer you can, even if it provides just small improvement in some unimportant job factors.

Patrick McCleod had been the strength and conditioning coach for an Ivy League college football team for a little over a year. After the third terrible season in a row, the new athletic director fired the longtime head coach and replaced him with a well-known former professional football coach. At their first staff meeting the athletic director and the new coach stressed that they didn't feel the need to make wholesale changes in the staff. "Stability" and "tradition" were important values of the university. The new head coach made a point of individually meeting with every member of the staff and asking him to stay. The new coach was a persuasive, charismatic individual, and Patrick felt tempted to believe him. Two other junior coaches whom Patrick was friendly with were convinced, and encouraged Patrick to stay on as well. Patrick, however, made it his business to line up another job as soon as possible. He found a job as strength and conditioning coach and head trainer of the lacrosse team at the nearby state university for an almost identical compensation package. Before the start of the next football season one of Patrick's coaching friends from the former job was demoted and the other was fired.

## Bill Kaplan Plans for His Next Job

Lucky for him, Bill Kaplan's job situation wasn't as unstable as Patrick McCleod's. Bill worked on developing a personal network, as I suggested, and began job fishing, looking for interesting offers. During his first year on the job nothing came along that provided more than improvements in unimportant factors. After eighteen months, however, that changed. Bill attended a fund-raiser for adult literacy at the local library. There he met and struck up a friendship with a well-known author. At a dinner party at that author's home, Bill met the owner of a special-interest bookstore. The two hit it off and the owner offered Bill the job as manager of the store, for a 20-percent salary increase. Bill took the job. Six months later he came to me for help in negotiating the future purchase of the store from the owner, who's planning on retiring in the near future. For Bill, the transition from uncertain college graduate to potential owner of a bookstore in just a couple of years has made him happier than he could have imagined. Firing his boss has turned his life around.

Firing *your* boss can turn *your* life around as well.

# CHAPTER 9

# The Life of
# Your Dreams

*I learned this, at least, by my experiment:
that if one advances confidently in the
direction of his dreams, and endeavors
to live the life which he has imagined,
he will meet with a success unexpected
in common hours.*

—HENRY DAVID THOREAU

YOU CAN INCREASE your income.

You can spend less time at work and more time at home with your family.

You can achieve the kind of psychological, emotional, and even spiritual fulfillment you've always wanted.

You can feel in charge of your work life.

You can decide when to leave your current job and have a choice of new job offers.

You can feel optimistic about your work future.

You can lead the life of your dreams.

You can achieve all of this by adopting the new set of attitudes toward work I've discussed and following the seven simple yet empower-

## THE FIRE YOUR BOSS PROCESS

1. Fire your boss . . . and hire yourself.

    a. Check your control over your work life.

    - What is your value in the workplace?

    - What kind of benefits do you deserve?

    - What skills do you have?

    - What do you consider your greatest achievement?

    - How long do you think you need to work at a particular job or task to master it and be ready to move on to another job or task?

    - Do you have a personal plan for your work life?

    b. Take charge of your work life.

    - Write your own job description.

    - Give yourself a performance review.

    - Define alternate courses.

    - Put your plan in writing.

2. Kill your career . . . and get a job.

    a. Why do you work?

    b. Come up with ways to get what you want, other than money.

3. There's no I in job.

    a. Figure out what your boss most needs and wants.

    - What does he do during the day? What does he get from it?

    - When does his mood change? Why?

    b. Is he one of the common types of bosses?

    c. Prioritize his multiple needs.

    d. Develop ways to meet his needs.

4. Go fish.

    a. Stay abreast of job opportunities.

- Note alternate and current paths.
- Determine top trade publications for each path.
- Find headhunters or employment agencies for each path.
- Compile reading and agency list.

    b. Go over ads regularly.

    c. Read publications regularly.

5. No one hires a stranger.

    a. Draw on existing personal network.

    b. Expand personal network.

- Dress and act appropriately.
- Ask questions, point out similarities.
- Be polite and offer help.

6. It's the money.

    a. Chart the twenty factors for each offer.

    b. Prioritize the important factors.

    c. Compare all the factors for each offer.

7. Hello, I must be going.

    a. Reanalyze current job factors.

    b. Prioritize factors again.

    c. Compare new offer factors.

    d. Determine timing for leaving.

ing steps I've outlined in this book. (See the box on page 198 for an outline of the entire process described in the preceding eight chapters.)

## The Seven Steps

Start by firing your boss and hiring yourself. Write your own job description, give yourself a performance review, define alternate courses for your work life, and put your plan into writing. This will let you take charge of your work life. On the outside you'll seem as loyal and subservient as ever, but on the inside you'll be charting your own course. You'll be able to figure out how much you're worth and what skills you need to add to your repertoire, and to choose short- and long-term goals.

> Remember Wendy Rosenfeld, the woman who had allowed her boss, a politician, to assume control over her work life? Wendy fired that controlling boss and hired herself. She took some college courses to expand her graphic and computer skills, and began fishing for work in corporate communications and not-for-profit development. After nine months of looking, during which she continued to efficiently manage her boss's campaign headquarters, Wendy landed a position as director of communications for an old-line social service agency in Manhattan. She felt secure enough to buy herself an apartment and start creating the kind of social life she never had when her former boss, in effect, dictated where she'd live and for how long. She's never been happier.

Next, kill your career and get a job instead. Analyze why you work. Determine ways to get what you want through areas of your life other than work. Then start pursuing those routes to fulfillment outside of work. Soon you'll achieve the satisfaction you crave and will have more time to enjoy it. Rather than trying to find work that fulfills all your wants and answers all your needs, divide your life into a work portion and a personal portion. Work will become less frustrating and life will become more satisfying.

That's what Sean Shanahan discovered. Having spent most of his working life as a designer, trying to combine art and commerce, Sean finally decided to kill his career and get a job instead. He turned what had been a home office into a studio to do his own art. By not placing the burden of providing psychological satisfaction on his work for the design firm, Sean found he didn't feel the need to spend so much time at the office, or bring work home. He started feeling better about work and about his personal life too. Sean entered some of his work in a juried show for the first time since college and received an honorable mention. Encouraged, he's now working on a new set of collages, hoping to build up sufficient work to interest a local gallery. He's now achieving the artistic fulfillment he always tried to get through work, through his personal life instead.

Then, realize there's no I in job. Focus on meeting your boss's needs rather than your own. That will let you secure your job even while spending less time in the office. It will enable you to earn raises and praise even though you're actively looking for another job. Determine what your boss needs and wants, by figuring out what type of boss he is and observing him carefully. Prioritize his needs and decide which to tackle first, and how. Then make him feel as if his success and happiness are your number one goal.

That's exactly what schoolteacher Janet Crosetti did. An ossi-
fied department chairperson was causing Janet many problems
upon her return to teaching. A cowardly boss, Janet's chairperson threatened to make her teaching job a potential minefield.
But Janet realized that the best way to make her own job safe
was to make her frightened boss feel safe. By playing to her
chairperson's ego, offering to accept responsibility for risks,
and warning about possible problems and offering solutions
ahead of time, Janet built a cocoon around her boss. After nine
months on the job Janet had moved from troublemaker to the
apple of her boss's eye. At the start of her second year the
chairperson was actively promoting Janet to the school administrators as a star in the making.

Your next step is to "go fish." That means learning how to go job
fishing rather than job hunting. Rather than reactively looking for
work when something happens at your current job, become a proactive job seeker who's constantly looking for another position. And instead of focusing on finding a job you want, concentrate on attracting
job offers whose merits you can judge after receiving them. Alternatively, offers can be used as bargaining chips to get more at your current job, or to create competition between two suitors.

Jared Edwards's sales career had been long and varied, but always reactive, until he started job fishing. Having gone
through a long and difficult time finding his current job, Jared
became proactive, actively seeking offers even though his job
was going well. He had received two offers in his first year of
job fishing but turned them both down because they didn't
pay enough. Jared then developed a connection with an
inventor-entrepreneur by using his fishing techniques. He

slowly cultivated a relationship with the individual. While this was going on, Jared picked up some preliminary signs of instability at work. Jared reeled his new contact in, and won an offer of a job that paid the same as his current position but offered the possibility of earning far more. He grabbed it after his current boss wasn't able to match some of the new opportunities. Three months after taking his new job Jared learned of wholesale layoffs at his former employer.

The fifth step is to realize that no one hires a stranger today. The age of networking and informational interviews is over. Draw on your personal relationships to find job offers. Make friends, not contacts. Socialize, don't network. Expand your personal life and you expand the universe from which you can draw connections, broadening your reach into fields and industries you'd never otherwise touch. Pursue those things you most enjoy in your personal life and you'll also benefit your work life.

Fred Peters, director of publications for an Ivy League university, was faced with an unsettled situation where he worked. In an effort to get away from the threatening departmental politics, Fred decided to start job hunting. But when he tried to use traditional job-search and networking techniques, he came up short. Fred learned that no one hires a stranger today. As a result he began expanding his personal life instead. Fred began playing more golf, joined the board of his son's youth hockey league, and even got active in local theater. Fred struck up a friendship on the golf course with the general manager of a printing company, which led to his being offered a new job as assistant general manager of the company's local facility. Six months since landing that job, Fred is sill working on expanding his personal life. He's joined a gym and a reading group, and is planning on taking an art history class in the spring. He's leading a richer personal life than ever before, and simultaneously expanding his job prospects for the future.

Next, accept that it's the money that counts when choosing which job offers you should take. Isolate the twenty factors that characterize every job. Prioritize them based on your current situation and future needs. Give maximum weight to those that provide you with more money or more time. Trade amenities, a comfortable environment, and a supportive culture for paid time off. Exchange status, title, and opportunities to advance for a higher income. Swap autos, retirement plans, and perceived stability for a shorter commute.

When Debbie O'Leary came to New York she had a hard time finding a radio job like those she'd held previously. In fact, she had a hard time finding any job. It took more than eighteen months, but Debbie eventually received two offers: one a part-time deejay position at a rock station, and the other a jazz-programming job for a satellite radio network. Debbie's instinct was to take the deejay job, since it offered status and opportunities for advancement as well as a comfortable environment. But after weighing the factors involved in both offers, she realized that the satellite radio job offered more opportunities for learning; a better retirement plan; and most important of all, considerably more money. A year after making her choice, Debbie feels even better about it. The satellite network is making inroads in the marketplace, and Debbie has gotten two bonuses. The radio station where she would have worked has gone through a format change, from rock to sports talk, meaning she would have lost her job.

Finally, you need to enter your job with a plan for leaving—an attitude I call "Hello, I must be going." Accept that no job is permanent. Resolve to leave on your schedule rather than your boss's. Turn leaving a job into a positive step rather than a defensive one. Determine what additional compensation will improve your situation, and then take jobs that provide it. Make a quick move to a new job if it's a major improvement. But after a couple of years make a move for any improvement to keep your forward momentum.

Bill Kaplan was excited to land a job as assistant manager of a bookstore after graduating college. Having had a nomadic academic and work life up until then, he found stability inviting. Yet, he soon realized he had to plan for leaving. Bill analyzed his current job and prepared a checklist against which to compare job offers. He began job fishing and expanding his personal network. Through his work for adult literacy, Bill met the owner of a special-interest bookstore who offered him a job as manager of his store. Since it represented a 20-percent salary increase, Bill took the job. After six months at the store the owner and Bill worked out a plan allowing Bill to purchase the store over a period of five years. With three years still to go on his buyout plan, Bill is as thrilled with the possibility as ever. At our most recent meeting he and I worked up a business plan for the store, including projections for when it should be sold. Bill is convinced of the need to always have an exit strategy.

You can turn your work life around and create the life of your dreams. I've been helping my clients do just that for the past three years. They've used the same process I've outlined in this book. It has worked for them and it can work for you.

## Breaking Free from the Doldrums

I know it may be hard to believe. Even after reading this far you may still feel that you've no hope. I know how hard it can be to overcome malaise and break free from the doldrums of the current work environment. I know how bad it is out there.

While all the Wall Street economists and Washington pundits talk about a recovery, it still feels like a recession on the sales floor, at the office, and in the factory. Both the clerk earning $12,000 and the executive earning $112,000 rightly feel their jobs are hanging by threads. In the face of this insecurity most of us are working longer hours than ever before. When people are laid off they face a lack of new job opportunities.

The average employee sees his income shrinking and his hours increasing. He's getting no satisfaction from his career. He feels his job is in jeopardy, and he has no control over his work life. The future seems bleak.

Then, in the midst of all this bad news, I come along and write that you can actually create the job of your dreams and lead the life of your dreams. I offer up examples of my clients and say you can do what they did. I suggest seven steps to follow that fly in the face of conventional wisdom, and make it all sound so simple.

That's because it is.

## A Change in Attitude

Turning your work life around isn't easy, but it is simple. The seven steps require considerable time and effort on your part. But when push comes to shove, the whole process really just comes down to a change in attitude. If I can get you to accept and implement just one thing from this whole book, it's this: you are not your work.

For decades we have all been trying to integrate our work lives and personal lives in an effort to create a wonderful holistic life. We've pursued careers we thought would make us wealthy materially and spiritually. In the process we've done immeasurable damage to our lives. We've been making presentations rather than baking cookies with our kids. We've spent time at sales conferences instead of soccer games. We've been staring at our computers rather than sunsets. We've gathered around conference tables rather than dinner tables.

Separating your self from your work doesn't mean giving up the search for material wealth. In fact, it makes it easier to achieve wealth. Stop looking to satisfy your own needs and start satisfying your boss's needs instead. You'll earn more and be more secure. Stop trying to climb a hierarchy and start looking for new jobs instead. You'll be in control and will find work more quickly.

Separating your self from your work doesn't mean giving up the search for fulfillment. In fact, it makes it easier to achieve fulfillment. Stop looking for joy at work and start looking for it at home or in church. Stop trying to make your work creative, or make creativity your work, and instead work at your job and create in your life. You'll find emotional, psychological, and spiritual satisfaction.

Some people have told me they think my Fire Your Boss philosophy is cynical. I couldn't disagree more. I think it's idealistic. It places the greatest priority on helping you achieve your dreams. Fire your boss and you'll finally be able to take charge of your work life. Fire your boss and you'll finally be able to find the fulfillment in life you've always wanted.

All it takes is a change in attitude. I'm asking you to take a leap of faith. To step away from the conventional and embrace the radical. I've led you to the brink of happiness. But you have to take the next step.

# PART II

# FIRING YOUR BOSS IN THREE COMMON SITUATIONS

The remaining three chapters show how the Fire Your Boss philosophy is applied in three work situations. I've always felt it important not just to write about what someone should do, but to show how to do it. These chapters are intended as supplements, not substitutes, for the previous chapters. They're written with the assumption that you've read the rest of the book and are coming to these chapters for help in applying ideas you've already absorbed.

# Firing Your Boss When You're Unemployed

*It's a recession when your neighbor loses his job;*
*it's a depression when you lose yours.*

—HARRY S. TRUMAN

IF YOU'RE UNEMPLOYED you probably wish you still had a boss you could fire. And I'm sure some of you can think of a lot of other things you'd like to do to your ex-boss besides terminating him. But the first thing you need to do is to get over your anger.

Many people who are unemployed have every right to be bitter. Since you were open-minded and proactive enough to pick up this book, and intelligent and determined enough to get this far into it, odds are you lost your job through no fault of your own. I know that's of little comfort. Neither is knowing that you're not alone. There are millions of other good, honest, hardworking, skilled people out there who are unemployed through no fault of their own. Misery may love company, but it's an affection that provides little solace and less empowerment.

The rage felt by some of those who are unemployed is understandable. But it's not very helpful. Anger is an impotent emotion: it doesn't do anything for you. In this case it's probably born of impotence as well: people are angry that others, not they, had control over their work life. It could also come from a sense of outrage. They held up their end of the bargain, but their boss didn't. They showed up on time, they did their job, perhaps they even excelled. Yet they got fired. Where's the justice in that?

Well, there is none. As I wrote earlier in this book, there is no justice in the workplace today. Believing otherwise often leads to disappointment. I hate to say it, but many of these people are right in feeling impotent. They had no control over their work life. They were nothing more than a budget line to be cut so someone higher up the ladder could keep his job for another couple of months.

Instead of getting angry, get even. How? There's an old adage that says living well is the best revenge. I couldn't agree more. Payback will come by your taking charge of your own work life, making sure you're never put in this position again, and getting to lead the life of your dreams. That's what I told Jason Hope when he came to my office.

A tall, thin man who looks a bit like Tom Hanks, Jason came to see me on the advice of a mutual friend. Jason was fifty-one, and had been vice president of sales and marketing for the U.S. subsidiary of a Japanese electronics firm for six years. He had spent his entire working life in the consumer electronics industry, starting out as a salesclerk in a retail store after college. From there, Jason became a salesman for an American company that made high-end audio speakers. After a half dozen years with that firm he became a regional sales manager for a larger American firm that made mass-market electronics products. Nine years later he became national sales manager of the Japanese firm, eventually being promoted into the position from which he was fired after more than a decade with the company.

Jason was able to negotiate a severance package that included six months' salary. That slowed, but didn't stop, his family's economic problems. Jason's wife, Beth, works as a dental hygienist at an office not far from their home in suburban New Jersey. They have two sons, Steve, a senior in college, and Tim, a junior in high school. Jason and Beth were astute enough to make some very quick adjustments in their financial lives. Beth was able to add Jason and their sons to her health insurance plan at work. They helped Steve obtain loans for his last two semesters in college that, while not subsidized, deferred repayment of principal until after graduation. They took out a home-equity line of credit, gave up one of their cars, and cut back on all their discretionary spending. Jason believed all this belt-tightening and his severance would help carry the family for the year he thought it would take for him to find another job. The plan would have worked, except after a year he still had no job in sight. Another six months passed before he came to see me.

Still seething over having been fired eighteen months earlier, and increasingly angry at himself for not having found a job sooner, Jason was right on the cusp of despair when he came to see me. I spent about fifteen minutes "talking him off the ledge." I explained that if he let himself sink into despair he'd signal that to the world and would have an even harder time getting another job. The antidote, I suggested, was to fire his ex-boss.

## Firing Your Ex-Boss

The first homework assignment I give to clients who are still employed is designed to get them to realize the degree to which they actually lack control over their working life. If you're unemployed you don't need my help in realizing that. However, you still need to break the hold your former boss and job have on your psyche and your self-image.

How are you determining your value in the workplace? I'll bet you're looking at what you were earning at your job before you were fired. I'll bet the same is true of what kind of benefits you think you deserve. Even though you've been fired, you're allowing your ex-boss to continue to define who and what you are. Use your termination as an opportunity to shatter those chains. Just because you were earning $90,000 a year at your former company in your former industry doesn't mean that's your value in the overall job market. Someone like you may well be worth $150,000. Or it could be your real value is actually only $75,000 today. Obviously it's preferable to find out you are undervaluing rather than overvaluing yourself, based on your previous job. But it's still better to find out your actual value is lower, and then land a job, than to continue to have an unrealistic view, and remain unemployed.

The same goes for the rest of your work image. Are you assuming a certain work path based solely on the path you would have followed if you'd stayed at your former employer? Are you stressing certain achievements in your past based on what your ex-boss valued? Are you viewing yourself, and describing yourself to others, based on the job description of a job you no longer hold? You are not your job. And you certainly are not your ex-job.

God knows there are a lot of bad things that happen when you lose your job. But just as every cloud has a silver lining, and the Chinese use the same character for "crisis" and "opportunity," so too can being fired have a positive element to it . . . at least if you're willing to get past your bitterness and embrace that chance. Being fired is an opportunity for you to break completely with your past. It's a chance to start over and carve out a new identity for yourself. It's a time when you can become who you want to be rather than continue being who your boss said you were. Don't let him continue his hold over you even after firing you.

My suggestion is to write a job description of the job you want, not the job you lost. What is it you are best at? Where do you feel you excel? What are your strengths? You know the answers to these questions far better than your ex-boss ever did.

After crafting your own job description, investigate its value in the marketplace. How? First, by consulting classified ads, reading professional journals, meeting with employment agencies, and chatting with headhunters. Then, simply by testing the waters. You are worth what the market will pay for you. Use your self-definition as the bait in your job fishing and you will soon learn what you're worth in today's market.

## Jason Hope Fires His Ex-Boss

Jason, despite his lingering anger with his former company, admitted to me he was continuing to define himself based on its perspective, rather than his own. At first the admission made him even angrier than he was. But after a few minutes discussing how he could now develop his own job description, Jason's anger abated and eventually morphed into excitement. His homework assignment after our initial consultation was to come up with that self-definition. Before he left he told me this was the first time he'd been excited about work in more than a year.

When he returned a week later, Jason seemed a different man. His anger was gone, replaced by enthusiasm. He had taken my suggestions to heart. He had sat down with his wife and gotten her feedback and insights into his work image. Their conclusions surprised him. Jason realized he had bought into the work path of his employers, rather than creating his own. While he excelled at personal selling, he had moved into sales management because that was the next step in the ladder at his company. Once on that path he never stepped back to reconsider his direction. In addition, he realized he was basing his ideas about compensation on just one industry. Jason decided he would seize the opportunity and redefine himself. Rather than marketing himself as a sales and marketing executive, he would promote himself as an expert at selling high-end consumer products to specialty retailers.

## Kill Your Career . . . and Get a Job . . . Any Job

It's surprising, but unemployment on its own doesn't seem to be enough to convince some people to stop looking for emotional, psychological, or spiritual fulfillment through work. I've met with people who, despite being out of work for more than a year, continue to look for work they believe will be more than just financially rewarding. When faced with a choice between going into debt or giving up the pursuit of "meaningful" work, they opt for debt. Sometimes they are enabled in this by "supportive" spouses or parents who are equally convinced of the importance of having a career as opposed to a job. In many cases, the longer these individuals hold out, the more they become committed to their cause. It's as if the only thing that can justify their prolonged unemployment is that they're on an almost spiritual quest. Then, rather than compromising on the psychic side of the equation, they compromise on the financial side. Eventually they take a job paying far less than they previously earned, far less than they could potentially earn, simply to ensure that their work is more than just a mercantile pursuit. Please, if you follow no other piece of advice I offer in the chapter, at least don't let this happen to you.

As soon as you can after being fired, do a self-analysis and try to figure out your reason for working. What is it you're looking for from work . . . besides money? Once you come up with an answer, immediately address that need through your personal life. If you want to be of service, go out and volunteer one evening a week, even if you're out of work. Feel the urge to be creative? Splurge on a set of water-colors and dedicate one afternoon on the weekend to painting, or do whatever it takes, within reason, to fill that artistic need. The sooner you address your psychic needs through your personal life, the sooner you'll be able to focus on just getting a job—any job—in order to generate a stream of income.

That's really the key: regenerating a stream of income as quickly as possible. It doesn't have to be a job with long-term potential. Feel free to minimize your experience if you think it will hurt your chances on an interview. If your motivation is questioned, say you've taken early retirement, or just came into an inheritance, or are thinking of changing careers, or want to get insights into a new industry or business. Say whatever it takes to get the job.

Having a stream of income coming in will do two things for you. First, it will relieve some of the economic pressure you're experiencing. Obviously this emergency income may not be what you were used to. But something is better than nothing. Remember, this is just temporary, and no honest labor is demeaning. Second, a stream of income, however small and whatever its source, will improve your self-esteem. Some clients don't believe me when I tell them that. But that's because they've never been out of work for a long period of time. I have. And I can tell you firsthand that your self-image takes a nosedive. Did it feel good for an out-of-work former CEO and banker to work part time teaching adult ed classes? No. But it felt better than not working at all, sitting home in my bathrobe feeling sorry for myself.[13]

If nothing else good comes from your being out of work for a time, at least you'll have finally put an end to this destructive pursuit of meaningful work. Once you discover you can satisfy your nonmone-

13. For the whole story of my spell of long-term unemployment and my road back, read my book *Second Acts*.

tary needs through your personal life, you'll be free to focus on working for the money.

## Jason Hope Kills His Career and Gets a Job

In the eighteen months since he'd lost his job at the consumer electronics firm, Jason's pursuit of meaningful work had abated, but not vanished. He admitted to me he still looked for more than just money from work. When I pressed him about what he was looking for, he had a hard time answering me at first.

We talked about his work life and the choices he had made. As we spoke it became apparent to Jason that he had always been looking for respect from work. He told me his parents had been disappointed that he never pursued a profession. His father, a career garment salesman, had made it clear he was upset that after graduating college Jason chose to get a job selling audio equipment. He told Jason that he hadn't sent him to college so he could end up being just a salesman like him. Jason said that, on some level, he felt his climb into management was at first done partly to gain the respect of his father. He added he probably still harbored some feelings that being "just a salesman" wasn't enough.

I said to Jason he clearly wasn't "just a salesman." He was a loving husband and father. He had been a Democratic committee person. Besides, there was nothing wrong with being a salesman. Just because his father felt inadequate was no reason he should. I suggested he do something else in his personal life that would provide him with the feeling he was respected. After a few moments' thought, Jason admitted he had been approached to serve on the board of his synagogue, but had hesitated because of the time commitment. I said maybe he should reconsider, and meanwhile, he should just look for a job—any job—to bring in some income and make himself feel a bit better.

A week later I got a telephone call from Jason. He had accepted a spot on the synagogue board. It meant a one-night-a-week commitment, but Jason admitted it gave his esteem a boost. He had also applied for a floor sales job at a local consumer electronics superstore. Jason didn't hide all his experience in the industry from the manager, but explained he had taken early retirement and was looking for something to "keep busy." He didn't explain that it was a forced early retirement or that he intended for it to be only temporary. While the starting salary wasn't even half what he had previously been earning, it would provide the family with some much needed financial relief. Both Jason and his wife already felt more optimistic about their lives and their futures just with the possibility of Jason's getting a paycheck.

## There's No I in Unemployment Either

Focusing on your boss's needs, rather than your own, is the route to success and increased security once you've gotten a job. But it also has an application if you're unemployed.

Far too many unemployed job seekers go into job interviews with the wrong attitude. Early in the process, still fresh from employment and confident you'll soon be back in the saddle, you may come off as overconfident. You may signal to the interviewer that the job in question maybe beneath you. I'm all for projecting confidence and making the interviewer feel like he must compete for you . . . when you've still got a job. In that situation your confidence is understandable. If you're unemployed and yet you're acting superior, you look conceited and maybe even a little out of touch. After not getting any offers for a few months people with such attitudes often shift to the other extreme. Desperate for a job offer, you signal this desperation to the interviewer. He's usually made uncomfortable by the excessive toadying and begins to suspect there's something wrong with you and that this, rather than market conditions, is why you've been out of work for so long.

The solution is to adopt a middle ground right from the start, and then maintain it throughout the process. You need to show an immediate interest in the needs of the interviewer and his company, rather than your own, and that you are ready, willing, and able to meet those needs. To paraphrase JFK, ask not what the company can do for you, but what you can do for the company. You'll have some initial hints as to what the company's or interviewer's needs are by the way the position is advertised or described and by the skills and experiences stressed. But the best way to find out exactly what's needed is simply to ask. Be direct and ask what the ideal candidate would provide for the company. Then show how you match that description. This two-step approach demonstrates an eagerness to please and self-confidence. That's a terrific combination.

Earlier in this book I wrote about how bosses will say one thing about what they want from employees, while actually wanting something else. I haven't changed my mind. That's still the case. But in an interview process when you're unemployed, it's essential that you buy into the charade. If you ask and the interviewer says he's looking for a straight shooter who'll be an agent for change, talk about your integrity and explain how your innovative streak will shake things up. Then, after you land the job and find out he really wants someone who'll protect him from *his* boss's demands for change, transform yourself into his stoutest defender. Believe me, he will never question the transformation. In fact, he'll thank his lucky stars for having found the absolutely perfect person for the job.

## Jason Hope Demonstrates There's No I in Unemployed

As soon as I heard Jason had applied for a retail sales position at the consumer electronics store, I suggested he make sure he maintained and projected the right attitude. He agreed, noting that he himself was worried about not being able to keep from showing how much more he knew about the business than the store manager, and acting as if the job were beneath him. We talked for a few minutes about how to keep the focus on the manager's needs.

The next day I got another call from Jason, letting me know he had gotten the job at the store. He said he directly asked the manager what he was looking for. The answer was someone knowledgeable about high-end audio equipment, who could relate well to customers, and was reliable. Jason told of his lifelong love of audio equipment and portrayed his long affiliation with the industry as having been as much hobby as work. He talked about having been successful in retail sales and about having learned a lot from all the retailers he had worked with in the past. Jason noted that since he was a close match to the demographics of the average customers, he shouldn't have a hard time relating to them. As someone with experience in business, he said, he knew how important it was to be on time and reliable. Jason was offered the job on the spot and told he could start whenever he wanted.

## Job Fishing for the Unemployed

The principles of job fishing are to look constantly for work and to concentrate on getting offers rather than on getting jobs. Once again, while I developed these principles with the employed individual in mind, they have relevance for the unemployed as well.

Some unemployed job seekers engage in what I call a serial job hunt. They find one or two potential jobs, or perhaps focus on a single industry. Then they follow through on those possibilities, to the exclusion of all others, until they are exhausted. If they don't land a job, they look for another industry, or find another couple of openings, and pursue these exclusively until they are exhausted as well. This kind of linear, systematic approach is almost guaranteed to increase the time it takes to find a new job. And it definitely guarantees that you will never be in the enviable position of having more than one offer to choose from.

That's why I encourage my unemployed clients to pursue as many leads as they can develop, all at the same time. Answer all the help wanted ads that fit. Contact every employment agency that seems a player in the market. Call every headhunter. Tap into every resource. Sure, it means having to keep lots of balls in the air at the same time. You'll need to keep track of where you've sent your résumé and when, whom you've contacted and met with, and whom you've e-mailed and telephoned. Since you'll be pursuing opportunities in different industries and of different types at the same time, you'll need to be able to switch hats quickly and have a conversation about the aerospace industry right after sending an e-mail to someone in the fast-food business.

I know this kind of multitasking isn't easy, but it is essential. If you don't know how to do this by the time you're unemployed, use the extra time you now have on your hands to become a master of it. You'll need it once you're back in the workplace. That's because from now on you'll be perpetually looking for work . . . unless you want to find yourself in this position again.

Rather than being selective about pursuing opportunities, based on prejudgments, go after every possible opportunity. The idea, whether you're working or unemployed, is to have multiple offers to choose from. Not only will having multiple offers give you a chance to pick and choose the one that's best for you, it will make you feel better about yourself.

## Jason Hope Goes Job Fishing

Even after Jason landed the job at the consumer electronics store, I urged him to keep on looking for job offers, wherever they might come from. He agreed and spent every Thursday afternoon—which was one of his days off from the store—answering ads, researching industries, and touching base with his business contacts. A month after taking the job at the electronics store, Jason was offered another retail sales position, this time at a camera store. He turned it down, but admitted it felt nice to be "in demand."

Jason also signed up with a temporary agency that specialized in filling executive positions. Seven months after starting at the consumer electronics store, Jason was offered a temporary position developing a marketing package for a health food supplier looking to expand into new retail markets. While he realized it wasn't a long-term solution to his situation, it would pay $20,000 more than he'd earn at the store. He took it . . . but still kept on looking for work.

## No One Hires an Unemployed Stranger

I believe it's vital for someone who's unemployed to work on expanding his or her personal network and use that as a source for job leads. I understand, however, that it's a far more efficient strategy when you're still employed and can give those new relationships more time to develop and turn into leads. That's why, if you're unemployed, I think you should look to bring in a stream of income as soon as you can, rather than waiting for the job of your dreams to appear. Grab a job that will help you keep food on the table and your head up. But keep scanning the help wanted ads in newspapers, on Web sites, and in professional journals. Keep hounding employment agencies and headhunters. Work your business network in the traditional manner. Yes, it's a real long shot these days, but you've nothing to lose other than the time it takes. If your fishing yields an offer that pays more than the job you took to keep food on the table, grab it, but don't stop fishing for other offers.

While you're working hard with all these short-term, traditional techniques, make the most of your personal life. Pursue your hobbies. Get active in the community. Volunteer. Do all the things you always said you'd do if you ever had the time. Well, you now have the time, so make the most of it. Not only will it bring you psychic benefits, but it's also probably going to be the way you find your best long-term job leads. Be inquisitive, interested, and optimistic. If you have a closed mind you'll end up facing only closed doors in your life. Keep an open mind and you'll find doors open for you, sometimes in the places and circumstances you don't expect.

## Jason Hope Expands His Personal Network

Jason kept up his job-fishing efforts after getting the temporary marketing job through the agency. In fact, knowing the position was temporary actually spurred him to step up his efforts. But he didn't let that interfere with the expansion of his personal network.

Jason took some woodworking classes at a local DIY superstore. He dusted off the classic Hasselblad medium-format camera he'd used years earlier and joined a photo club in order to make use of its darkroom facilities. He continued on the board of his synagogue. Jason and Beth both joined the high school football team's booster club, since they went to most every game to see their son play. Surprisingly, it was at a football game that his personal network first began to pay off.

The booster club member who handled the PA announcements at the games couldn't make it one day, so Jason volunteered to take his place. Up in the tower overlooking the field he introduced himself to the man who was the regular spotter. It turned out this fellow, Sal Yamen, was a longtime friend of the coach of the football team. Jason and he got to talking during breaks in the game, and they hit it off.

Sal was the owner of a company that imported and distributed toys. While his company handled a wide variety of products, what he was most excited about was a line of highly detailed figures based on movie, comic-book, and sports heroes. The figures were more sculptured miniatures than action figures, and Sal planned to sell them through comic-book stores, hobby shops, and sporting-good stores. Jason told Sal about his experiences selling and marketing to specialty dealers in the consumer electronics industry. The two agreed to go out for drinks after the next week's football game. That meeting led to a more formal lunch and follow-up conversation at Sal's office. And that eventually led to Sal's offering Jason a job as national sales manager of the new product line. The idea was for Jason to personally lead the sales effort nationwide, and to train the existing sales staff, who were used to toy stores, to service the accounts. It wasn't the kind of offer Jason had been expecting would come along.

## It's the Money . . . Now, More Than Ever

Someone who's employed has the luxury of picking and choosing when to take another job. She can analyze the twenty main elements in each job offer she receives, focus on the important ones, and weigh whether or not to accept the new offer. When you're unemployed you lose some of that luxury. The secret to having some choice in the matter is to approach offers realistically as early in the process as possible.

I've found that many unemployed individuals start their job search being too discriminating and, after spending an uncomfortably long time in a fruitless search, become too willing to settle. Early in the process, flush with whatever severance pay was received, and perhaps energized by outrage and the desire for revenge, job seekers set their sights high and either ignore or turn down offers that fall below either the income or the status level of the job they held previously. Then, if they remain out of work, there's a tipping point in the process when suddenly their optimism turns to pessimism. Their severance may be gone, their savings used up, and their credit lines tapped out. Outrage is no longer expressed as revenge, but as fear and desperation. They take any job they can find. With their confidence at a new low, their finances shot, and their family's patience and understanding eroded, they feel compelled to stick with the job they took in desperation for far longer than they should.

My advice to clients, and you, is to be more realistic from day one, and accept that when you're unemployed it really is the money that matters most of all. Remember, your choice isn't between your own job and the new offer or opportunity you're considering; it's between unemployment and employment between some money coming in and none. If you reach this conclusion early on, you'll be able to target the best-paying of the opportunities available. For example, you'll take the job as an office temp as opposed to the job as a waitress, the job as a manufacturer's regional sales rep instead of the job as a retail salesperson.

I would suggest giving yourself two weeks of full-time traditional job hunting to find a position similar to the one you just lost. If there's a big demand for your experience and skills you'll see that within two weeks. If you don't get interviews within two weeks, lower your sights, find the best-paying options that *are* readily available, and grab one.

With that income coming in you'll have the time to start job fishing. You'll also be in the position of now being able to weigh any offers you receive against an alternative: your current job.

What's essential is that you compare any new offers to the job you currently hold, not the job you were fired from. That job is gone. Using it as a template against which to compare new opportunities will only prolong your unemployment. Ironically, I've found that the earlier my clients get reemployed, even with a job at a considerably lower income level than the one they previously held, the sooner they end up returning to that higher income level. It seems that it takes less time to take a step or two backward, and then another step or two forward, than it does to move forward from the dead stop of unemployment. People who are working seem to attract new job opportunities.

## Jason Hope Realizes It's the Money That Counts

While Jason enjoyed meeting with Sal and discussing the opportunity in the toy industry, he still felt some hesitation about taking the job. I asked him if the job with Sal's company would pay more than the temporary marketing job he currently held. It did . . . quite a bit more actually. It wasn't located as near to his home, but it provided far more paid and unpaid time off. And it certainly gave him a chance to learn some new things. So what was the problem? I asked. Jason said it didn't pay as much as his job with the electronics company, and, truth be told, he didn't think the toy business was as prestigious as the consumer electronics business.

I waited a moment, thinking how to answer. But then I realized it was best to be direct. Jason was a big boy and he'd shown himself to be resilient and strong. I told Jason he didn't have a job in the consumer electronics industry, earning six figures; he was working as a temporary marketing executive for hire, earning considerably less. The choice wasn't between the job he'd lost and this new one; it was between the job he had and this new one. It was time to stop looking backward and start looking forward. Jason said he appreciated my being blunt. He said he guessed he had to "bury" his old job. I agreed, but told him not to look at this as the end of something old, but the beginning of something new.

## You Must Be Going Again . . .
## but on Your Own Schedule

No one is more aware of the transitory nature of employment today than someone who has just been fired. And no one should be more determined to make sure he takes charge of his future leaving.

It's vital that you not let reemployment cloud your vision. No matter how much better you feel about yourself, regardless of how much more humane your new boss seems, you were still hired to be fired. This is the way the job world works now, and the sooner you accept that and come up with ways to deal with it, the less likely you'll be to experience unemployment again in the future.

Keep looking for work, even though you've got a job. Remember the rules I outlined in chapter 9. If you get another offer that represents an improvement in two important factors (income, proximity, paid time off, unpaid time off, or opportunities for learning, or perhaps health insurance, disability insurance, life insurance, tuition reimbursement, or retirement plans), grab it, regardless of how short a time you've been at the other job. If you've been at a job for between a year and two years, grab any offer that's an improvement in just one of your important factors. And after two years on the job, take any offer that represents any improvement at all.

Don't think that you're damned to change jobs every two years for the rest of your life. If your current job continues to offer more than the alternatives out there, that's great; stay there. But the moment it doesn't offer more is the moment you should move on.

## Jason Hope Sets His Own Schedule

Jason knew his job with Sal selling the toy figures wouldn't last forever. One of the things he and Sal had in common was an understanding that the consumer product business today was inherently unstable and insecure. Today's hot toy or electronics product in a specialty store was destined to become tomorrow's loss leader at a discount store. Sal said all he hoped was to be able to keep riding the wave for as long as possible. Jason agreed. For him it meant that he'd have to keep on looking for work, albeit primarily through his personal networking, even while trying to build up the new product line across the country. And if he found a better job, he'd take it.

But as he and I discussed, that wasn't such a bad prospect when you analyzed it. He had a nice steady income. His work was actually interesting, since he was learning something new. Besides, he was back taking photos again. His woodworking classes hadn't turned him into a master carpenter, but he was able to redo the molding in his den. The high school football booster club had asked him to become the full-time announcer the next season, his youngest son's senior year. He had gotten a lot of kudos for his work on the synagogue board. When he looked at his life, rather than at just at work, he realized he was actually a lot better off now than he had been before he was fired. He was back working again . . . and this time he was working to live, rather than living to work.

# CHAPTER 11

# Firing Your First Boss

*If* A *is a success in life, then* A *equals* x *plus* y *plus* z.
*Work is* x, y *is play; and* z *is keeping your mouth shut.*

—ALBERT EINSTEIN

SOME OF YOU entering the job market for the first time are probably wondering how long you have to pretend to read this book before
you can hand the book back to your parents, thank them, and then go
on doing exactly what you intended before they tried to offer you advice, through me. Some of you may even have turned to this chapter
first as a shortcut rather than reading from the beginning as your folks
suggested. If you fall into either of these categories I'd like to make a
deal with you. If reading the next three paragraphs doesn't convince
you to continue on to the end of the chapter, you can go ahead and quit.
It will be our little secret. But in return, if you find the next three paragraphs intriguing, you have to promise to finish the chapter. At that
point, you can decide whether or not I know what I'm talking about and
if it's worth your time to go back and read the book from chapter 1 on.

Everything your college career office told you is wrong. Interviewers and recruiters couldn't care less about your grades; your class rank; or in most cases, the college from which you graduated. In most cases, it's who you know, not what you know, that counts. How did your teachers and advisers get things so wrong? Well, in the first place they're working in an academic environment rather than the real world. Academics have no idea about practical things. Unlike everyone else in the working world, they have tenure, meaning the only way they get fired is if they commit a violent felony. There's an old adage that says, "Those who can't do, teach." In many cases that's true: some of your professors couldn't succeed in the real world and so they retreated to the safety of the academy. In other cases your professors never even tried to succeed in the real world: they stayed in the theoretical world rather than venturing out into the practical one.

The nonacademic staff who work in the career office *have* to tell you that your grades and your rank are important, and that a diploma with your college's name on it is particularly valued. Why? Well, the college has been trying to convince you to work hard for those grades and that rank. If it tells you that, upon graduation, no one will care if you had a 2.7 or a 3.9 GPA, it won't be able to convince you to work hard. The college has also been taking a lot of money out of your pocket for four or more years. If it told you that, other than in a few rare cases, the college from which you receive a diploma doesn't matter in the real world, that would fly in the face of its charging you all that money. The aim of the career advice you get from a college is to make sure you keep working hard and paying your bills, not to help you get a job.

If you go out and look for work in that meaningful career you've chosen, you're going to end up just like your parents, working longer and longer hours; earning less than they'd hoped; having no job security; and feeling emotionally, psychologically, and spiritually unfulfilled. They entered the job market with the same idealism and enthusiasm as you have right now. They shrugged off their own parents' warnings and concerns. The last thing they wanted was to replicate their parents' work lives. Well, they got their wish. Your parents got to lead work lives different from their parents': work lives that were less satisfying and fulfilling. Your parents gave you this chapter to read, not because they think they know best. They know they *don't* know best. They know they made mistakes that led to unhappiness and dissatisfaction with their work lives. Your parents don't want you to make the same mistake they did. They want you to fire your boss before you even get hired and start your work life fully in charge of your present and future. Besides, your youth and inexperience can actually be helpful in some elements of the radical approach to the job market I advocate. That's what I explained to Liz Mandel when she first came to see me.

Liz is a twenty-one-year-old recent college graduate. Her father, Don, is a high school principal who went to college with one of my children. Her mother, Jacquie, is a math teacher at a private school. A very petite redhead, Liz looks younger than her age, despite her very fashionable dress and appearance. After doing very well in her suburban Long Island high school, Liz went to a well-respected private university located in Manhattan. Her family had too high an income to obtain much financial aid or get many subsidized loans, but not enough savings or liquid assets to be able to pay the very large tuition bills. As a result, Liz took out a series of unsubsidized loans that she had to begin paying off upon graduation.

During her sophomore year Liz decided to become a philosophy major. She had always loved attending religious services, not only of her own faith, but of all faiths. Her parents used to joke that they wished she asked uncomfortable questions about sex, like other kids, rather than asking all those uncomfortable questions about the meaning of life. Liz loved her philosophy classes, and also loved participating in a variety of different political and service organizations while at school. At the beginning of her senior year she had decided she didn't want to go to graduate school . . . at least not right away . . . but instead wanted to work for a nonprofit organization that either helped the poor or was a force for social change. Having lived in downtown Manhattan for four years while in college, Liz was determined not to have to return to her parents' home on Long Island after graduation. She had a friend who was willing to share the costs of an apartment, but when they investigated rents in Manhattan she was shocked. When her parents heard about Liz's plan to work for a nonprofit and get an apartment "in the city," they resisted the urge to try to talk her out of it, but couldn't resist asking me to speak with her.

When we had our initial conversation, I explained to Liz, much as I explained earlier in this chapter, that her parents' motivation was to ensure that she didn't make the same mistakes they had and end up getting neither psychic nor monetary fulfillment from work. While she was a bit resistant at first, Liz was open-minded enough to listen to me when I suggested she needed to fire her first boss, even before she knew who it would be.

## Firing Your Boss Even Before Getting Your First Job

You have a wonderful opportunity to start your work life off on the right track. Most people, from their first job right out of college to their last job before retiring, cede control over their work lives to their bosses. They allow their bosses to determine their value in the workplace. The skills they pick up throughout their working lives are determined, not by which are potentially the most lucrative or important in the long term, but by what their boss needs them to do in the short term. After just a few years of workplace subservience people's perceptions of their achievements, value, and abilities become shaded by their bosses' judgments. Instead of having their own proactive plan for their work life, they become reactive and let their bosses determine the course of their work life.

Firing your boss means taking charge yourself. For you, that means developing your own work profile and plan even before you get your first job. The idea is to have an intelligent, cogent, self-generated answer when someone asks, "What kind of work are you looking for?"

Start by coming up with a one-paragraph job profile: a description of the type of work at which you think you'd excel. Don't worry about things like titles or industry specifics. Instead, focus on verbs: action words that describe the mental and physical aspects of a job. For instance, you might conclude that you'd excel at a job that involves writing and communicating. Or perhaps you think your strengths would be in researching and analyzing. Maybe you feel you'd be best at developing and organizing. Put your profile in writing.

Next, conduct a brief "performance review" of your past. What was it that led you to select those verbs when developing your job profile? Did you have your greatest academic successes in, let's say, science projects where you were responsible for researching and analyzing information? Was your prime role in your summer job writing and communicating information for your local newspaper? Were your extracurricular and personal activities centered around developing and organizing, perhaps by launching and leading a charity drive? Make note of the results of your review, writing your findings beneath your job profile on the same sheet of paper.

Take a few minutes to read over your profile and review. Refine it, if necessary, or tinker with the wording. Make it as concise as possible. You want to be able to convey this information in one or two conversational sentences.

## Liz Mandel Fires Her Boss Before Getting Her First Job

It didn't take much convincing for Liz to see the advantages of taking charge of her own work life right from square one. Both her parents had often complained about the extent to which their work lives were controlled by their bosses. Her father, even though he had finally become a principal, had spent years having his work progress blocked by the combination of an incompetent principal and a domineering superintendent. Then after a shake-up in the school board led to his finally getting the principal's job, he found his powers strictly curtailed by a block of board members who had engineered the ouster of the previous principal and superintendent and who now sought to micromanage the entire district. Liz's mother had been made to teach seventh-graders rather than the younger students she preferred, and had been told to go back and get additionally certified in social studies rather than biology, as she'd wished. Both felt they'd given up control over their work lives years ago. Both were also working hard to regain it, however, by having me help them fire their bosses.

At the end of our first session together I asked Liz to go home and work on her profile and review. She called me the next day to tell me she'd done some thinking and thought she had it worked out. Thinking back over her academic career, Liz decided she was very good at analyzing problems, finding a variety of potential solutions, and then analyzing the pros and cons of each option. Most of the jobs Liz had held up to now were doing light filing, data entry, and answering telephones, so they didn't really apply to her job profile. But her academic work in philosophy certainly did, as did some of her extracurricular activities. In high school she had trained as a peer counselor, and then in college she had volunteered at a suicide-prevention hotline. She had come up with the following answer to the question of what kind of work she was looking for:

> My strength is in problem solving. As a philosophy major and a volunteer crisis counselor I learned how to isolate problems, research possible solutions, and analyze the alternatives.

## Killing Your Career Before It Even Starts

If you take only one thing away from this chapter, I hope it's this: you are not your job. I believe the single best way to ensure that you earn a good income *and* get some level of psychic fulfillment is to abandon the notion of being able to achieve both through work. The focus of your work life should be to earn money, while the focus of your personal life should be to provide you with emotional, psychological, and spiritual satisfaction. By splitting your life in this manner you vastly improve your chances of being happy.

I know this doesn't match up with what most of you have been taught or told. That's because most of the people offering you advice are baby-boomer academics. When your parents' generation was young they thought such a divided life was a terrible idea. Their goal was to lead a holistic life in which work and personal life were inextricably and harmoniously linked. It was a very idealistic theory. For academics it was actually possible. But everyone else has discovered that it didn't work in practice. Most of the members of your parents' generation ended up working ever increasing hours at jobs with ever decreasing security, for incomes that didn't keep pace with inflation, and in the process they've become more and more dissatisfied with their lives. Both their work lives and their personal lives are actually less fulfilling than those of their own parents. You won't hear this from your college advisers, since they've remained sheltered from real-world market forces. You will hear it from your parents . . . or at least see its evidence. My goal is to keep you from falling into the same trap.

I'm advising people to kill their careers and get jobs instead; to work to live rather than live to work. Careers are supposed to produce psychic as well as financial reward. Jobs are simply tools to make money. It's very hard for some of my older clients to make this transition. They've spent years struggling to achieve their dream of a rewarding holistic life. If they give up now they're forced to admit all that effort and time were wasted. Still, most are biting the bullet and killing their careers. That's because the result is getting what they most want: a happier, more fulfilling life. I'm hoping you won't waste years of your own working life in the pursuit of a nearly impossible dream, making yourself miserable in the process. Unless you're going to spend the rest of your life in academia, I'm urging you to kill your career now, before it's even born. You won't regret it.

At this stage in your life the process will actually be quite simple. Think about what, besides money, you most want from work. Do you want to be of service, or to express yourself? Are you looking for status, security, or respect? Or is your goal to travel or meet people? Whatever it is, you can more easily achieve it through your personal life than through your work life, particularly at your age. Right now you have fewer obligations and responsibilities dictating what you need to do with your personal life than you will when you grow older. That makes this the perfect time for you to seek out and pursue those things that provide the psychic satisfaction you crave. Now, before you have children, is the time when you can spend multiple evenings a week playing with a chamber music group. Now, before you have household chores, is the time when you can spend all day Saturday working with a church youth group. Now, before you have multiple schedules to coordinate, is the time when you can spend two weeks hiking through Scotland. As you grow older you'll need to make more compromises and sacrifices to achieve the kind of personal satisfaction you crave. Now all you need to do is abandon the notion of career and embrace the concept of job instead.

## Liz Mandel Kills Her Career

Before she met with me, Liz had planned to look for work with a not-for-profit agency or organization that worked on behalf of the poor. From an early age she had felt the need to serve, inspired by her parents' examples. This drive to serve meshed with a strong spiritual element to her life. While both her parents were spiritual in their way, they weren't religiously observant. Liz, on the other hand, took a great deal of comfort from religious worship. Unfortunately, her drive to serve didn't mesh well with her desire to carve out a life independent of her parents. Right after college Liz and a former college roommate began scouting for an apartment they might be able to afford on their projected incomes. While certainly not spoiled, Liz had grown up in solidly middle-class environments. However, the areas of New York City where she could afford to live if she took an entry-level job working at a not-for-profit agency were, to use her roommate's euphemism, "authentically urban."

It was at this point that I introduced Liz to the idea of killing her career and getting a job instead. I thought she'd reflexively resist the concept, but after only a few moments' thought she seemed to see all its advantages. After about ten minutes she was already talking about ways she could express her need to be of service through volunteering, and ways she could follow up on her religious impulse as well. By the end of the dialogue she was genuinely excited about killing her career.

## There's No I in Your First Job

A key element in both landing and keeping a job today is realizing there's no I in job. That means focusing on your boss's needs and wants rather than your own, or the company's. Once again, as someone new to the job market, you have some advantages.

Having spoken about this concept with a number of young clients fresh out of college, I've learned that this is similar to a technique many savvy students use to ensure they get the best possible grade in a class. Rather than approaching the material in an entirely objective manner, these ambitious students study the professor's statements and writings to determine his or her own preferences and prejudices. Then the students package and present their work in a manner or style that mirrors the professor's own ideas or approach. These clients of mine also report that college professors are no different from bosses in that they almost universally seem oblivious of such efforts.

Another advantage you have as a neophyte job hunter is that it's easier for you to determine a boss's needs or wants. When anyone applies for a job, the secret to determining a boss's superficial needs and wants—those he openly talks about during the search process—is studying the ad and drawing inferences during the interview. As a young person you can be completely direct and simply ask, "What are the traits you're looking for in a candidate?" Whereas such a direct approach would make an experienced job hunter appear naive, it's refreshing coming from a young person. Bosses love young subordinates to be eager, obedient disciples. Directly ask what you can do and you'll not only gather the information you need to present yourself in the best light, but you'll also score bonus points in the process.

Once you're on the job it will become apparent that what the boss said he wanted from a candidate during the search process is different from what he wants from an actual subordinate. Here's another place where you have an advantage over more seasoned employees. They need to study and observe their boss's behaviors to figure out how best to meet his needs. You can simply ask, "What can I do to make your work easier?" Again, your directness and obvious eagerness to please will be a plus. Having been told what you should do, all that's left is for you to do it.

## Fishing for a First Job

I tell my clients they need to go job fishing rather than job hunting. Instead of waiting until they're in dire need of a new job, and then going out looking for a specific type of job, like some kind of big-game hunter, I think people today should act more like a fisherman. That means constantly looking, regardless of how long you've been at a job, and focusing on landing as many offers as possible, not necessarily looking for a particular job. The idea is to cast a wide net and regularly land a large catch of offers from which you can pick and choose.

For a first-time job seeker this means being as open-minded as possible about which opportunities to pursue initially, and pursuing a large number simultaneously. One of the things you may not have learned in college is the ability to multitask. You may have been able to go to one class at a time, and to do your work one project at a time. In the job market you'll need to be able to juggle multiple projects in which you may play different roles. Your first lesson in this will be to not look for work in a serial manner. Too many young people, uncomfortable with the process, send out a mass of résumés, land perhaps one or two leads, and then pursue those leads until they yield either a job or a rejection. In the latter case they start the process again, sending out a mass of résumés, getting a couple of leads, and following them to their end. Instead, you need to be constantly sending out résumés and constantly pursuing leads. You need to always be doing every step in the process.

Just as important, when you find a job, you need to keep job fishing. Most people end up in industries or professions by default. Fresh out of college they get a job in, let's say, the greeting card industry. They stay with their first employer as long as possible, perhaps getting one or two promotions. After just a couple of years they feel they've made an investment in the industry, and that their best chances for finding another job are to stick with it. So they keep looking for work in the greeting card industry. By the time they're in their thirties they're considered "industry veterans." Not only are they afraid they won't earn as much, or be able to maintain their organizational rank, if they shift industries, but they're secretly worried they won't be able to cut it in another industry. Greeting cards are all I've ever known, they'll think to themselves. I can't leave the industry. By continuing to look for another job, even after landing your first job, and taking a better offer as soon as it comes along, you'll be able to avoid falling into that trap.

## No One Hires a Young Stranger Either

You're entering the job market at a time when the standard job-search strategy no longer works. For years, most people in business eschewed classified ads and instead drew on a business network consisting of coworkers, peers, clients, customers, and competitors to generate job leads. They'd use their network to gather names of people with whom to hold informational interviews: overtly casual conversations to get advice, but covertly requests for jobs. The lack of job growth and a push by human resources professionals to regain control of recruitment and hiring has led to the demise of networking.

I'm urging clients to instead return to the use of help wanted ads, since they are the single best way to get a job, any job, in the shortest period of time. For many, that's what's most important. But I'm also suggesting that my clients follow a second, parallel path by tapping into their personal lives for job leads. That's because no one hires a stranger anymore.

Since, as a newcomer to the world of business, you don't have a network on which to draw, its demise as an effective job-search tool isn't an issue. Luckily you do have a personal life you can use to generate job leads.

However, since most of your social contacts are probably people in situations similar to your own—just entering the job market, returning to a hometown after four years away, or making a fresh start in a new community—they may not offer either the breadth or the depth of social connections that could generate job leads. That's why you need to follow a slight variation on the technique I outlined earlier in the book. You need to tap into what I call your "second-generation social life."

Instead of looking to your friends or to people you've met in social situations for job leads, look to other people's social contacts. Ask your parents and older siblings to tap into their social lives for help. Anytime you're invited to meet friends' parents, grab it. Invited to a party at your parents' neighbors? Leap at the chance. Is your aunt begging to take you to church with her to show you off to her friends? Do it. Don't look at going to the Rotary Club breakfast with your father as the equivalent of having teeth pulled. It's an incredible opportunity to tap into a social sphere that could yield multiple job leads.

A second-generation social life has an added bonus. You will be one of the only young people present. As such you'll stand out and attract attention. Instead of seeming like a desperate job seeker, you'll appear to be a young person with an unusually mature approach. Just your presence at these kinds of events will create a positive perception in the eyes of others. Whenever the people at that Rotary Club breakfast are told about a job opening for a young person, they'll instantly think of you.

## From Day One, It's the Money

When you do get that call from a Rotarian about a possible job lead, it's vital that you realize which characteristics of a job are important today, and which aren't. Most of the people who follow the Fire Your Boss approach will analyze the twenty main elements in each job offer they receive, focus on the important ones I describe in chapter 7, and weigh whether or not to accept the new offer. When you're just starting off you'll do the same, but some of the elements carry a slightly different weight.

The unimportant factors are the same, whether you're getting your first job or your fiftieth: amenities, auto, challenging, culture, environment, expense allowance, opportunities for advancement, stability, status, and title. The factors I believe are definitely important remain that way as well: income, proximity, paid time off, unpaid time off, and opportunities for learning. It's some of the questionable factors that, I believe, take on increased importance for those getting their first job. Disability insurance, retirement plans, and life insurance, while potentially valuable to some, aren't always essential to first-time job seekers. On the other hand, health insurance and tuition reimbursement, I believe, are definitely important factors for someone getting his or her first job. Let me explain.

Most young people fail to realize how expensive health care can be. Having been covered by your parents' health plans up until now, you've probably never received a bill for medical services. The response from most young people, when faced with the possibility of having to pay large medical bills because they don't have insurance coverage, is to go without care. That's an understandable response. However, it's not a wise one. The only reason I don't consider health insurance coverage an important factor for all of my clients is that many of them can obtain coverage from a partner, and so can do without coverage of their own. Since most first-time job seekers aren't yet able to obtain coverage from a partner, my recommendation is to consider health insurance coverage one of the important factors in choosing a job.

For most of my clients tuition reimbursement is an important factor only if the selection of courses isn't limited. That's because most experienced job seekers are returning to college in order to acquire skills and credentials that will allow them to more easily enter a different industry or profession. For a first-time job seeker, further education is almost always a good thing. My suggestion is that you should add tuition reimbursement to your list of important factors.

All that being said, the most important factor, whether you're just entering the job market or are getting your final job before retirement, is still the money.

## You Must Be Going, Even Though You Just Started

When you land your first job you need to enter it with the attitude that it's only a matter of time before you leave for another job. That's true for every worker, but it's especially true for the first-timer. Don't let yourself get too comfortable. This is an excellent opportunity to set a pattern for the remainder of your working life: that you, rather than your boss, will determine when and how you leave your job.

In order to determine whether or not it makes sense to leave your current job for another one, you need to weigh the twenty elements that constitute each job offer. I tell my clients that their decision about leaving should also be influenced by the length of time they've held their current job. For instance, if you've held a job for a year or less, you should leave for another only if the new position represents an improvement in at least two of the factors you consider important. If you've held a job for between one and two years, you should leave only if the new position is an improvement in at least one important factor. And if you've held a job for more than two years, you should feel free to move for any job that offers a boost in any of the factors, important or not.

However, if you're in your first job I think the rules should be slightly different. I believe a first-time job holder should be ready to move within a year for any position that represents an improvement, even if it's just in one important factor. In addition, if you're still holding that initial job after two years, I'd suggest you take another, even if it doesn't offer an improvement in *any* factor, but simply is a change. I believe it's essential for young people to create a momentum in their work lives and to fight any tendency toward complacency. In the twenty-first century, movement is essential for a successful work life. The sooner you learn that and make it part of your life, the better.

## Liz Mandel Lands Her First Job

After accepting that she needed to kill her career before it even began, Liz set aside her idea of getting an entry-level job in the non-profit sector. After speaking with a former professor about her desire to find a volunteer activity, Liz contacted a neighborhood youth center in Brooklyn. She and the director struck up a quick friendship, and Liz volunteered to help set up a peer counseling service. Liz also decided to go "temple shopping," as she called it. After attending services at a number of synagogues around the metropolitan area, Liz found a small but energetic Reconstructionist congregation in Manhattan that seemed to provide much of what she was looking for in a religious community.

While she was busy creating a fulfilling personal life of her own, Liz tapped into the personal lives of her parents and her friends' parents, looking for job leads. It was actually at a barbecue in her parents' backyard that she struck up a conversation with a neighbor she hadn't seen in years. A marketing executive in the sporting goods industry, he had started consulting with a large national chain of sports stores that was setting up an electronic commerce operation. After hearing Liz explain how studying philosophy had taught her how to be a problem solver, he mentioned that that was exactly the skill the sporting goods store's e-commerce arm was looking for in staffing its customer service department. The chat at the barbecue led to an office meeting, followed by an interview.

At the interview Liz saw that the hiring manager seemed to be looking for people who would be compassionate with customers. Liz stressed not only her problem-solving skills, but also her charitable work. She got a job offer. Since the only other offer she had was for an entry-level position at a bookstore, and that paid much less, Liz took the customer service job. After a few weeks on the job Liz quickly realized her boss's real need. A veteran in the retail business, he didn't have much of a handle on the Internet customer. But he was being pushed by the management of the new e-commerce operation to come up with innovations. Liz began offering suggestions and new ideas he could use. Within six months she was promoted to be his deputy.

Despite her promotion, Liz continued to fish for other job offers. After a Bible study group at her synagogue, she and a very fashionably dressed woman in her midforties struck up a debate about Spinoza. It

# CHAPTER 12

# Firing Your Boss in Another Industry

*To betray, you must first belong. I never belonged.*

—KIM PHILBY

THE ONLY THING separating most businesses from each other is jargon. Sure, there are fields requiring specialized technical knowledge, like auto mechanics and neurosurgery, but most industries have far more in common with each other than most people realize.

Businesses usually follow similar sets of strategies and employ comparable arrays of tactics, regardless of what they're actually selling. That's actually the first common point: all businesses are selling something, even if it's intangible, like advice. I know it's something of an oversimplification, but you could say there are only three business strategies: sell the best for the most, sell the cheapest, or sell the best compromise between quality and price. In addition, all your skills and experiences in business operations can probably be divided into three categories: finance, management, and marketing.

turned out that the woman operated her own business running focus groups for clients. As I was in the process of writing this chapter, Liz was in the process of talking with the woman about a possible job facilitating focus group discussions.

Before I met Liz I was worried that a young person who majored in philosophy wouldn't be pragmatic. She proved I was falling prey to stereotyping. Liz Mandel, a philosophy major fresh out of college, is as savvy and successful a practitioner of my Fire Your Boss approach as any of my most seasoned, bottom-line-focused clients.

The secret to successfully changing industries is realizing there's this similarity between businesses and then being able to demonstrate that sameness to others. You need to demonstrate that your skills and experiences are transferable. The first step in doing both is firing your boss and hiring yourself.

That's what I told Jody Harkins when she came to see me. Jody is the thirty-nine-year-old deputy director of planning and development for a small city in the northern suburbs of New York City. Married with two young children, she was referred to me by her brother-in-law, an attorney with whom I've worked on a number of different projects. Jody found herself in an all too common position. A bit of an obsessive, Jody hated to see anything left undone. She instinctively filled any vacuum she came across. I've found that, as if by magic, people like Jody always end up working for individuals who are more than happy to let others do their job for them.

Jody's boss, the city's director of planning and development, was a fifty-one-year-old former architect who cut a dashing figure at public meetings. Tall, distinguished looking, and the possessor of an aristocratic New England accent, he seemed to attract cameras. He did nothing to discourage the attention. That wouldn't have been a problem for Jody, who didn't like attention, except that his doing nothing extended to work as well. He was constantly traveling to conferences, attending seminars and meetings, and going out for long lunches, leaving Jody to do his work as well as her own. Jody had, without knowing it, successfully found and met her boss's needs, ensuring her security.

That security didn't outweigh two other factors. First, Jody had grown tired of playing her political role. She had become the public face of development in the city, despite her being the person that carried out rather than set policy. The politicians who did set policy were happy to have any angry citizens take their ire out on Jody. After a couple of very contentious projects she had wearied of that role. Second, Jody's earnings potential was limited. Not only were any salary increases subject to the vagaries of politics, but because her boss was a fixture in the director's position, Jody would never be able to rise above a certain income level. Her boss was open about his plan to retire from this position. (Behind his back Jody joked that he'd actually already retired.) Shifting to a similar job in another municipality would have required uprooting the entire family, something neither Jody, her husband, nor their children wanted to do. Jody decided that meant either sticking it out or changing industries. At a recent family gathering Jody had told all this to her brother-in-law, who suggested she get in touch with me.

## Fire Your Boss in a New Industry

In order to make the jump from one industry to another, you're going to need to take charge of your work life. If you allow your current boss to continue to define who and what you are, you'll never be able to break out of that mold and step into an entirely different industry. Most people have let their boss not only determine what they're worth, but also define their set of skills and plan out the course of their work life. Unless you break these chains you won't be able to convince anyone you're also able to break into a new business.

The way to do that is to write your own job description. What's important is that it make no reference to your current job, industry, or business. That sounds difficult, but all it takes is some thinking outside the box. Rather than focusing on your role in a hierarchy, think about your role in a process. How would you explain what you do to someone who knows nothing about your industry? Think about what you actually do during the day. Then write down all the verbs that came to mind. Using words like "analyzing," "organizing," "planning," "leading," "coordinating," and "communicating" will make it easy for people in other industries to understand what you do. To make the parallels even clearer, weave those verbs into one or more of the three business disciplines: marketing, management, and finance. By looking at your work in this generic fashion, and coming up with a way of communicating its universal nature to others, you'll be able to shift from any industry or business.

Let's say you are the editor of a newsletter for a museum. Your boss might say your job description is to develop the editorial calendar, set the freelance budget, write and edit the copy, hire photographers, supervise the design, and even oversee the printing and circulation. To someone outside of the publication business all this is just jargon. But what if you write your own job description, focusing on verbs and how the job fits into one of the three business disciplines. The new description might be that you "develop and supervise the creative and financial aspects of an ongoing marketing campaign designed to generate repeat business from past customers." That's a description that works for any industry.

## Jody Harkins Writes Her Own Job Description

Having spent almost all her working life in government, Jody initially had a difficult time translating what she did into generic business language. Jody's role was to be the generator, as well as the legal, physical, and aesthetic gatekeeper of any development in the city. Her job included trying to attract private developers to do business in the city, winning grants for public development, and overseeing the planning of the actual projects, making sure they met the city's requirements. She was the liaison between developers and the city, as well as between the city and its residents.

After a few minutes' conversation, Jody and I realized her job was actually a sales and marketing position. She not only prospected for new customers, but having found them, she provided customer service. In addition, she helped those customers in marketing to end users. Setting aside all the technical elements of her position, she was actually a full-service sales and marketing consultant.

## Killing Your Career and Getting a Job in Another Industry

One of the most common misconceptions I see in clients who come to me for help in changing industries is the belief that shifting industries will provide the psychic rewards they're missing. The failure to get emotional, spiritual, and psychological satisfaction from work has nothing to do with the nature of the work you're doing; it has to do with the nature of work itself. Expecting to get both financial and psychic rewards from work is the problem. That's true whether you're working as an actor or an actuary. Change industries with the idea that you'll find satisfaction in another business and you'll just find the same frustration you're feeling now. Remember: psychic rewards should come from your personal life, not your work. Your goal in changing industries should be to improve your work life.

## There's No I in Jobs in Any Industry

Another mistake I've seen made by many people who are looking to change industries is to forget that landing and keeping a job require a laserlike focus on a boss's needs rather than your own. A natural tendency of someone changing industries is to concentrate on one's own achievements and how they can be translated to the new industry. The problem with this is that you become the starting point for the argument for why you should be hired. Instead, your potential future boss's needs are where you should begin your argument. Don't take your own skills, abilities, and achievements and say, "Here's what I can do; now let me show you how I can do the same for you." Instead, find out what your future boss needs, and explain how you can fulfill those needs. You dialogue should be: "I understand you need x, y, and z; here's how I can provide them for you."

## Job Fishing in Another Industry

The challenge of job fishing in an industry in which you're not currently working is that you need to wear two very different hats at the same time. Normal job fishing requires you to keep meeting your boss's needs while pursuing leads for future jobs. While this means dividing your time and perceived loyalties, you are speaking one language, and keeping in touch with the developments of one world. Job fishing in another industry requires you to speak one language and stay on top of developments in one world while meeting your boss's needs, and to speak another language and stay on top of the news in another world while looking for new potential jobs. That's a more demanding task. My suggestion to clients is to create a schedule that allows them to change worlds. Usually I suggest they begin by devoting weekends, or one day a week, to their efforts at job fishing in their new industry. Obviously this may mean it will take longer to attract job offers in a new industry than it would in your current industry. If for some reason it's important to make the change quicker, you can simply devote more time to your future world. There is a trade-off to this, however. The more time you devote to your future world, the less secure will be your place in your current world. This balancing act has to be a custom job, based on your specific circumstances.

## No One Hires a Stranger from Another Industry

Tapping into your personal life rather than your business network is, I think, a much better way to find job leads in an industry in which you're not working. That's because your personal life provides a much broader range of people than your business network and, as a result, offers more possible connections to individuals indifferent industries. The secret is to make it clear during your social interactions that you're interested in the industry in question. When people ask about your work, mention your current business but quickly segue into a conversation about the industry you're trying to enter. To the best extent possible, make your proposed change of industry the prime topic of your conversations. Ask your acquaintances if they've changed industries, or know anyone who has. Seek out advice and opinions. The more enthusiasm and excitement you show about this new industry, the more feedback you'll get and the more leads you'll uncover.

## It's the Money . . . but Maybe Not Right Away

While it should remain your goal to select a job offer based on how it measures up in the factors you've deemed most important, changing industries requires a bit more flexibility. In order to get a position in a different industry, you may need to accept an offer that doesn't represent an improvement in any important factor. Before you do this, make doubly sure you're changing industries for long-term material benefits, rather than any perceived psychic benefits. I'd urge you, during your first year of looking for a new offer, not to accept any that represents a decrease in any important factor. A decrease in an unimportant factor is okay, however. If, after a year of looking to change industries, you still haven't received any acceptable offer, then I think it's time to consider taking a position for, let's say, less money than you're earning now. This may be one instance when you'll need to make a short-term sacrifice for a long-term gain. You may need to take a step backward today to be able to take two steps forward in the future. Just make sure that you do indeed take steps forward from this point on.

## You Must Be Going . . . but Maybe Not Just Yet

I encourage my clients who've taken a new job to continue to look for another position, but not to accept any offer within their first year unless it is an improvement in at least two important factors. After one year on the job I suggest that they accept offers that are an improvement in one important factor. And after two years, I believe, they should take any offer that's an improvement in any factor, important or not. When you change industries I think you need to be more selective, at least temporarily. In order to cement your change of industries in the mind of future bosses, I suggest you not accept any offer in your first year in a new industry unless it's an improvement in *three* important factors. No future boss would second-guess a move in that case. Similarly, after a year in the new industry I'd suggest you accept only offers that represent an improvement in two important factors. And after two years in the new industry I'd suggest you shift for any improvement in any factor, important or not. Two years is more than enough time in today's job market to make you a veteran.

## Jody Harkins Changes Industries

After developing her own job description, Jody and I discussed her plans for changing industries. She explained to me that she loved horticulture and had always dreamed of working in a nursery or garden shop. But when we explored that idea it became clear that her dream of working in a nursery was based on her drive to be creative, which she loved to express through gardening and landscaping. I suggested that she devote more of her personal time to tending her own garden, and perhaps even taking some additional horticulture classes, and focus on changing industries for material reasons. Jody understood my point and admitted that she and her husband had discussed other industry-change options, particularly her going to work for real estate developers. Jody realized that by, in effect, changing sides in the real estate development process and working for the real estate industry rather than a municipality, she could earn a great deal more money. At the end of our first session together I asked Jody to come up with some ideas for how she could meet the needs of her potential future bosses.

When she returned for our meeting a week later, Jody had prepared a memo for me about meeting future bosses' needs. She wrote that real estate developers needed to be able to anticipate and work to avoid the possible objections of community officials and residents. Her experience at working on the side of municipalities would be invaluable. Jody and I then discussed how she should conduct her job fishing. Knowing it would be difficult to look for work in the real estate industry while continuing to work for the city government, Jody and I agreed she should spend one day each weekend researching and exploring opportunities in real estate. We also talked about how she would use her social life to help look for job leads. Jody decided to get more active in the local Rotary Club. She had been sent to France on a Rotary-sponsored student exchange in high school, and felt a deep loyalty to the organization and its missions. She was already a regular churchgoer, and had decided she would get even more active, volunteering to serve on the parish council. Jody also said she had signed up for a bonsai class and had taken a plot at the community garden to give her more ground for her landscaping hobby.

After six months I got a call from Jody asking for another appointment. She told me she had been discussing her desire to change industries in her social life and that she had actually met the wife of a real estate consultant at her bonsai class. The consultant met with Jody and, over lunch, actually offered her a job. The problem was it didn't pay any more than her current job. She and I agreed that after only six months, it didn't make sense for her to make the jump just yet. Still, the offer had brightened her spirits and improved her self-image immeasurably.

At the time this manuscript was being finished, Jody was still job fishing. Her job with the city was as secure as possible, since she continued to assume much of the grunt work her boss avoided. Her personal life had yielded some additional leads. At church one Sunday, another member of the congregation introduced Jody to her nephew, who was one of the principals of a real estate development firm that was working to bring a megamall to a nearby city. She and he hit it off right away, and they've arranged to meet for lunch. I've told her I think it's just a matter of time until she's successful in shifting industries.

# INDEX